1295

D1570821

THE NEW
COMPLETE BULL TERRIER

The author with Ch. Madame Pompadour of Ernicor. "Pompy" was the Isis Vabo Trophy winner for 1949. She was Best Bull Terrier 80 times, a world record in her day, and defeated more competitors in the Terrier Group than any Bull Terrier before her. She died in 1960.

THE NEW COMPLETE
Bull Terrier

by
ERNEST EBERHARD

Second Edition
Illustrated

1978—Fifth Printing
HOWELL BOOK HOUSE INC.
730 Fifth Avenue
New York, N.Y. 10019

WRITING of the Bull Terrier in an article in *Popular Dogs* in December 1931—almost thirty years before President John F. Kennedy's famous inaugural address—Mrs. Drury L. Sheraton told this story:

> A friend of mine has two dogs; one is a Bull Terrier. She said to me one day: "My other dog looks at me and says, 'What have you got for *me?*' But my Bull Terrier looks at me and says, 'What can I give *you?*' "

Contents

Cover Portrait: Ch. Madame Pompadour of Ernicor.

Mrs. Ernest Eberhard with "Pompy".

Preface

ALTHOUGH I first owned a Bull Terrier around 1908, it was not until some twenty-odd years later that my then newly acquired wife and I became interested in showing and breeding them. The show bug bit us when we were induced to exhibit at a somewhat informal show and our six-months-old son of Ch. Comfey went best of 56 Terriers. He was good.

About two months later our winner went sour as a show dog, even though as a companion he proved to be the best dog we ever had. I naturally wanted to find out why such a promising show puppy had become such an utter failure. The people who had little success in breeding were most liberal in giving me information which, thank heavens, I had sense enough to realize was probably suspect. Otherwise, wouldn't they have been breeding better stock? The more successful breeders were reluctant to stick their necks out as far, but what they did say was of real value.

Books of the day did not give much help since they, too, often contained what were obvious fallacies. Over a period of years, I became convinced that in Bull Terriers we badly needed a book that would clarify the very things I was so painfully trying to learn about type and breeding. Therefore, when the opportunity came to

7

head the Publication Committee of the Bull Terrier Club of America to get out an Annual, I was most happy to seize it and to turn it into the book *Bull Terriers of Today,* which really delved into type. It was quickly sold out, with hundreds of orders left unfilled, including more than 200 from England.

It seemed obvious that the same kind of thing was needed on other phases of interest to Bull Terrier owners. A practical book was called for that would not only discuss in a popular way the basic principles of breeding as discovered through scientific experiments, but would also present the experience of the Bull Terrier breeders who had continuously shown their ability to breed the top ones. In addition, it would provide an extension of the studies on type made in *Bull Terriers of Today,* furnishing information heretofore not available in any book on the breed.

Hence this book.

No book which seeks to blaze a path can escape being controversial. Be assured however, a basis of the experience of many breeders lies in back of every statement I have made; nothing is based solely on one personal opinion.

When a subject is approached from several angles, as is done in this book, and the results all hang together reasonably well, the presentation ought merit careful and unprejudiced study. I, therefore, sincerely hope that *The New Complete Bull Terrier* will help toward an understanding of why some breeding programs are not proving more successful and what should be done about them, of how to select the sires and the dams most likely to produce top stock, and of how, either in the judging ring or out of it, to evaluate dogs in their proper order of excellence, to the end that both breeding and judging may be upgraded.

For their help with the book, I owe thanks to many. Above all others, to my wife, bless her, for seeing to it that my scribblings were made intelligible.

For their cooperation in providing material, I wish to express sincere thanks to the officers and members of the Bull Terrier Club of America. Warranting special appreciation are: Dr. E. S. Montgomery, former president of the Bull Terrier Club of America, for his help in reading the proofs of the first edition when—because of a stroke—I was unable to do so myself; Harry L. Otis, O.D., also a former president of the parent club, for providing important statistics; David Merriam, former president of the Golden State Bull Terrier Club, for the many hours he spent tracing down the Challenge Cup winners for us, and his summation of the American show scene through the 1960s; Raymond H. Oppenheimer, who in addition to the chapters duly noted in the text, provided pictures of English winners that are simply invaluable, and who furnished us a listing of all the Regency and Ormandy Jug winners; Mrs. M. O. Sweeten, editor of the *Bull Terrier Club Bulletin* (England) for allowing us to quote that valued publication; and the American Kennel Club, for their cooperation in promptly providing us with information on the parent Specialty and Best in Show winners.

And, in closing, a toast to "Pompy" watching over me every moment throughout her life.

—Ernest Eberhard

Ch. Romany Righteous Wrath, C.D., V.G., an outstanding English show and Obedience star of the mid-50's, pictured clearing a 9-ft. jump. He had to his credit a phenomenal jump of 15 feet. Bred by Miss Montague Johnstone and Miss M. Williams.

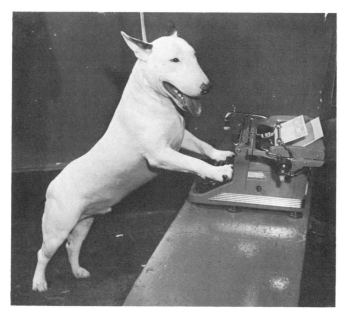

Davy Crockett of Ernicor types out the good news following his win of Best of Breed at Westminster 1956, at only nine months of age. Bred, owned, and exhibited by the author.

Exhibiting the Bull Terrier's adaptability with other pets is Bodger, one of the stars of the movie *The Incredible Journey*. His companion is the Siamese cat, Tao. (Disney Productions).

1

The Bull Terrier as a Personality

BULL terriers have brains, a sense of humor, imagination, personality. The Bull Terrier is more of a person than he is a dog and, if properly developed, will show mental qualities of a high order.

I recall one dog, Dapper Dan, a big son of Ch. Comfey, who I took with me for a walk on a farm. We came to a big haystack covered by a tarpaulin. I thought it would be fun for him to climb to the top, and gave the order. He made a flying leap to the tarpaulin, only to slip back off its slippery surface. He stood there for a moment obviously sizing up the situation. Then he made another leap. As he landed and started to slip back, he caught the tarpaulin with his teeth, hunched his rear legs up under him, made a grab at a higher place, and so inched himself up!

I was out with the same dog and two puppies one day, walking alongside a busy boulevard. One of the puppies slipped his collar and started to run. It seemed almost a certainty that he would be killed in the heavy traffic. Dapper, a powerful dog, broke away from me and herded the puppy back as expertly as if he had trained all his life for that moment. Yes, the Bull Terrier has brains. And he knows how to use them in an emergency.

We had a bitch, Betsy Ross, whom we shut up in the bedroom one afternoon while we went to the movies. When we came back, we found that she had opened the closet door, pulled out my traveling bag, jumped up on the bed with it (no mean feat in itself), pulled the zipper open, and had not only taken everything out but also had opened every case. The comb was out of its case, my razor was out of its case, and likewise my travelling slippers and everything else. All had been spread in a circle in the midst of which lonesome Betsy had gone to sleep. Who could scold her?

At that time, there lived next door a large and rather scrappy Boston Terrier. One day, as Betsy and I went back to the garage, the Boston jumped her. Betsy flipped him upside down, wrapped her front paws around him, and just held him helpless until I came up and rescued him. And quite pleased with herself she was.

The Boston was obviously sure that his foot must have slipped or something and so when another chance presented itself, he tackled her again. Once more she just flipped him upside down and held him helpless. A third time the dog tried his luck, and again Betsy flipped him. But this time she was beginning to lose patience and, as she held him, she let off a series of growls that must have instilled him with fear, for he never bothered her again.

Betsy did have a repertoire of growls that I have never heard equaled. It came about in this way. She was a six-months-old kennel puppy when we bought her, and the ways of the outside world were frighteningly strange. At shows she would crouch in her stall and, although she showed well in a pose, her movement was badly affected by lack of confidence in herself.

When she was about a year old, she was at a show and was benched next to a bitch that kept growling at her. I was coming back to the bench when Betsy noticed me some distance away. A most shamed look spread over her face, for she knew her cowardice was wrong, and she let out a weak sort of growl at the bitch next door, who stopped growling. Betsy perked up immediately. At the next show, the first thing she did was to growl at the dog in the next stall—who shrank away from her. Now she was on top of the world. After that, at every show to which we went, she would first growl at the dogs on either side and then, having told them off, would settle down.

These growls are no ordinary thing, but were the result of planned thinking. At home, one day, I heard Betsy growling terrifically. I peeked into the room and saw her sitting all by herself on the sofa. She would let out a blood curdling series of growls, then cock her head as if she were listening to herself. She kept that up for at least ten minutes, after which a satisfied look spread over her face as if she had come to the conclusion, "Well, that's it," and then she jumped off the sofa. I don't know the meaning of the growls she had been practicing, but they certainly were an effective bit of dog talk, as she proved time after time.

More than once I have noticed this ability of the Bull Terrier to prepare for the future. One day I had five of my dogs out together for a frolic, when a fight started between a 56-pound male and a 33-pound bitch, Virginia Dare. How it started I don't know, but the big fellow had her down. The two were moving so fast that I fell down three or four times before I could get hold of him and pull him off. Poor Ginny was full of blood, so I picked her up and carried her home. But when I washed her off and looked for the wounds, there weren't any. She had moved so fast on her back that the big fellow had been unable to grab her, and all the blood had come from him.

For several weeks afterward whenever Ginny played with her sisters, she played upside down, something she never had done before. It seemed obvious that she was preparing herself for an upside down style of combat. After about six weeks, she went back to her normal way of playing.

Time went on, until one day at the dinner table I dropped a napkin. Ginny sniffed at it. In a flash the big fellow was on her with a rush that carried her a good ten feet over against the wall. I dashed over, but could not get the big fellow to let go despite the fact that he had been trained to drop anything immediately. Finally I got them separated—and saw it was *she* who had grabbed *him*. Her hours of practice had paid off.

This big dog was one whom I could not break of fighting with our own dogs, as he was reluctant to obey when I called him. Finally, I had an idea, for I felt there must be a reason for his disobedience. Instead of calling him, I would call the other dog. He

A rare photo of General George S. Patton, Jr. emerging from a conference with Third Army unit commanders during World War II, with the real-life "Willie" (for William the Conqueror) at his side, as always.

In a moment's rest between scenes during the filming of "Patton", star George C. Scott and featured players Paul Stevens and Bill Hickman relax with Abraxan Aran, who portrayed "Willie". Actually there were two dogs used for the filming. From photographs of the real Willie, the filmmakers had to duplicate the General's "aide" twice because of quarantine regulations. One Willie had to be found for location shooting in Spain, and another later for filming in England. (Courtesy, Twentieth Century-Fox Film Corporation.)

Among others of prominence in public life that owned Bull Terriers were two United States presidents. President Theodore Roosevelt's "Pete" nearly caused an international incident by taking a healthy nip at French ambassador Jusseraud. Woodrow Wilson became the proud owner of a Bull Terrier presented to him by H. C. Hollister of Mobile, Alabama. It had appeared at some shows, and from its pictures appears to have been quite a good animal.

15

Bull Terriers like to make themselves comfortable, and often are as relaxed as a cat.

would then make no move to do any harm. After all, when I told him to stop and it was the other one that wanted to fight, why should he just stand there and allow himself to be bitten? Once I learned that secret, we had no more trouble.

We have been singularly free of fights between our own dogs and in the over fifty years since I first owned a Bull Terrier we have never owned a dog who has seriously hurt another dog or who has killed a cat. Our dogs have never been sissies—but they have not been encouraged to fight and they have been kept under control.

I recall a story told about Ch. Maldwyn, a big, 60-pound Bull Terrier. His mistress owned a Pekingese, which insisted on fighting with the big boy. Finally he lost patience with the little dog and picked it up in that big jaw that could have bitten it in half, and dropped it in the wastebasket unharmed.

I saw somewhat the same thing happen in the home of the Sheratons, who had two Bull Terriers, a Welsh Corgi, and a Peke, all living together. The Peke bit the Bull Terrier on the lip and hung on. The Bull Terrier walked over to Mrs. Sheraton and stood in front of her as much as to say, "Would you please take this excresence off me?"

The Bull Terrier has a remarkable ability to keep his head under all conditions. One time while we were asleep a little bitch we had jumped up on the bed. A big dog we owned decided to share in the comfort and apparently jumped on her accidentally. At any rate, she grabbed him and I was awakened by these two fighting dogs

16

barging across the bed. I thrust out my hand and my arm went between them. Both grabbed me and left their teeth marks on my flesh, but neither broke the skin. I have had that same sort of thing happen two other times. It is perfectly amazing how the Bull Terrier keeps his head under excitement and what wonderful physical and mental control he has.

It is that sort of sixth sense of his which makes him so reliable with children, who so often do not realize how much they may hurt a dog. With the Bull Terrier, if the child goes too far, the dog will get up and walk off.

William E. Schratwieser, one of the old-timers, told me about a bitch he had sold to a family with children. Since this family was pretty well off and had many toys, their garden was a rendezvous for the children of the neighborhood. The children and the Bull Terrier would play together in complete peace and harmony unless one of the children tried to take a toy off the property. The Bull Terrier would then go after the child, knock it down, and take the toy away. The children thought it great fun to test the bitch by trying to sneak away with a toy, but none ever managed to do so. Bull Terriers have a great sense of ownership and a common sense protective instinct that makes them invaluable as a family dog.

We had one big fellow who had quite a sense of humor, even though he often displayed it in a manner that was not too comfortable for the subject. When we had dinner guests, if there was a stranger present, the dog would sit and stare fixedly at him. The dog looked mean and his constant unwinking stare was enough to get on one's nerves. The guest would try to bribe the dog with tidbits from the table; the dog would take them but look as if he would prefer to have a bite of the guest. There was no friendliness in the dog until dinner was over. Then he would walk over to the guest, put his head on his knee, and look up with a most roguish expression as if to say, "Well, I put one over on you, didn't I?" For the rest of the evening, the dog would go out of his way to be friendly and when the time came for the guest to leave he had conceived a great admiration for the dog and his cleverness.

We had somewhat the reverse happen with one very lovely bitch who had a wonderful disposition and was friendly with everybody. From the time she had been a puppy, she had been quite friendly with a man who worked for us. Suddenly she turned against him, but only in one room in the house. When he worked there, she would go for him. The situation became so bad that every time he had work to do in that room, we would have to shut her up. When we did that, we soon noticed that our stock of liquor was decreasing at an alarming rate. We then put a lock on our liquor cabinet, after which we had no further trouble; the bitch never bothered him again. How she knew it was proper for him to touch anything in the house except our liquor will always remain a mystery to me, but she realized that this was our property and that he was not supposed to touch it.

Everybody who ever met our Madame Pompadour thought highly of her friendliness not only with people but with other dogs. Because of that, I was much surprised when at a Dog Week show in which she was invited to participate, she made repeated efforts to grab the dog benched next to us every time his head went near me. And she meant business, there was no mistake as to that. Later in the day I understood—the dog had to be taken off the bench because it had tried to bite several people. Pompey had realized the danger and, despite her inherent friendliness, was ready and willing to do what she could to protect me.

In my earlier show days, I saw a man looking at my dog and when I walked up he could tell by her immediate reaction that I was the owner. He said to me, "That is one breed of dog I would never own." Naturally, I asked him why, as he was the man who was judging the Terrier Group that day. His reply, and a very sincere one it was, "They get under your skin too much, and you feel too badly when they check out." His eyes filled with tears as he told me about the death of his Bull Terrier. He was a man around dogs enough to become calloused, but, somehow, one never gets calloused toward any Bull Terrier one has owned.

The last year of his life, Dapper Dan would become suddenly pensive and look at me with a sad expression. Then he would come over impulsively, give me a gentle kiss, and look at me as if to say, "Who is going to take care of you when I am gone?" He had a presentment—and yet they say dogs know nothing of death. He may not have known what death was, yet he knew we were going to be separated and it worried him. He was no show dog, but I still feel sad whenever I think of the passing of a dog who was a great friend.

18

The salute to the Bull Terrier by Willard Mullin, recently honored as "Sports Cartoonist of the Century", which appeared in the New York World-Telegram at Westminster time in 1937. The J. J. Johnston referred to in the title was then fight promoter at Madison Square Garden.

The old-fashioned Bulldog. The one at left is "Rosa", whelped about 1819 and considered the ideal until 1894. At right is "Crib".

Three English Terriers, "Silvio", "Serpolette" and "Salford".

2

The Bull Terrier and His Times

LIKE most breeds, the Bull Terrier has a sporting past which developed from the needs and fashions of days gone by. Badger and bull fighting were common amusements in the days when humans made a holiday of executions, when cruelty not only to animals but also to other human beings was the natural thing.

The Bull Terrier was developed from a variety of breeds into a dog with great virtues that were prostituted by the baser instincts of those who bred and owned him. His courage was proverbial, his endurance and resistance to pain unbelievable, and his intelligence was almost uncanny. These virtues, which we admire in both humans and animals, made him a great fighter, so much so that he is remembered as a fighter rather than for his other sterling qualities.

There were two other attributes which the Bull Terrier possessed above all rivals and which not only added to his value as a fighting dog, but also remain today to make him an ideal family dog. One of these was the ability to solve new problems and to think for himself in case of emergency. Once in the pit, the dog that could not solve a new attack died. The other quality was that under pain and excitement the Bull Terrier would not lose his head and bite his master when being separated from another dog in the pit. Added to these attributes is a craving for human companionship, a friendly love for all people and especially for his own particular family. These qualities make him not only unusually reliable with children, but also a companion and protector who can be depended upon in any emergency.

The Bull Terrier of today has retained the great physical and mental qualities of his redoubtable ancestors, but he has largely lost the instinctive combativeness of early days. It is the other dog who is generally most willing to start a fight, but it is the Bull Terrier who is least willing to quit. I have owned Bull Terriers for over sixty years, yet I have never had one of my dogs seriously hurt another dog or kill a cat.

Birth of the Breed

It was in the early part of the nineteenth century that the breeding of the basic Bull Terrier was started. At that time, an improvement in Terriers generally was being sought and new types were being developed. For fighting purposes, a cross between the Bulldog and various types of Terriers proved to be outstanding. The cross generally retained the courage and dogged determination of the Bulldog but added the speed, agility, and quick thinking of the Terrier. On the whole, these old-time dogs were a blocky-headed, ill favored looking lot and were to be found in all colors including white. They came to be known as the Bull and Terrier.

As time went on the Terrier characteristics became more noticeable. Heads were sharpened and legs were lengthened. White as a breed color became more frequent and was much admired. When James Hinks, a dealer of Birmingham, England, introduced his pure white strain at a show in 1862, the colored dog fell into disrepute.

There is no doubt that it is to this James Hinks that we are indebted for the more elegant dog who graced the latter part of the century. Robert Leighton, in Cassel's *Book of the Dog*, 1907 edition, states:

> These Birmingham dogs showed a refinement and grace, and an absence of the crooked legs and colored patches, which betrayed that Hinks had been using an outcross with a White English Terrier. . . .

Bull Terrier in armor at the Museum of the John Woodman Higgins Armory in Worcester, Massachusetts. Old time war dogs were thus protected.

Many persons objected that with the introduction of new blood he had eliminated the pugnacity that had been one of the most valuable attributes of the breed. But the charge was not justified, and to prove that his strain had lost none of its cherished quality of belligerence, Hinks matched his forty pound bitch, Puss, against one of the old Bull faced type (a sixty pound bitch) for a five pound note and a case of champagne. The fight took place at Tuffers in Longacre and in half an hour Puss had killed her opponent. Her own injuries were so slight that she was able to appear the next morning at a dog show and take a prize for her good looks and condition.

We find that some illuminating comments on the birth of the Bull Terrier were published in the now extinct American magazine *Dogdom*. These were written by James Hinks, son of the James Hinks previously mentioned. Mr. Hinks wrote:

The forbears of my father's dog presented a comical appearance with their short thick heads, blunt muzzles showing a certain amount of Bulldog layback, bow legs, thick-set bodies and overhanging lips, whilst in colour they varied between black and tan, brindle, red, fallow, etc. They were known as Bull and Terriers, owing to their being a cross between the Bull Dog and a Terrier, the latter being chiefly the large Black and Tan Terrier, and any Terrier which showed gameness and a nose for rats was used in the crossing. They were queer looking dogs, being neither Bull Dogs nor Terrier; however, they served the purpose they were bred for, i.e., fighting, ratting, badger and bull baiting. . . . The cross was ideal, as the strength of

23

Madman, probably whelped in the late 1860s, the first great Bull Terrier sire. Bred by James Hinks.

the Bull Dog was united with the quickness and intelligence of the Terrier.

Around the end of the fifties a great change came about. My father, who had previously owned some of the gamest of the old stock with which he had been experimenting and crossing with the White English Terrier and Dalmatian, bred a strain of all white dogs, which he called Bull Terriers, by which name they became duly recognized.

These dogs were refined and their Bull Dog appearance being still further bred out, they were longer and cleaner in head, stronger in foreface, free from lippiness and throatiness and necks were longer; they became more active; in short they became the old fighting dog civilized, with all his rough edges smoothed down without being softened; alert, active, plucky, muscular and a real gentleman. . . .

The Bull Terrier, although classified as a Terrier, should not be judged on Terrier lines, but by the Bull Terrier Standard correctly interpreted. In comparing dogs of the past with those of the present, the latter have a more uniform type of head, but there is a tendency to get the dog too leggy, and they do not stand so firm on the ground as did the oldsters.

24

Carleton Hinks, grandson of the original James Hinks, adds a bit on how the breeding was done (*Annual,* Bull Terrier Club of England, 1955). He states, "After many trials and disappointments he took to very close breeding, father to daughter, mother to son, the cry being to save the puppy with the most white."

In those early days pedigrees were a most mixed up affair. It is impossible to tell exactly what breeds were mixed together to form the Bull Terrier. However, it is quite well established that the old-fashioned Bull Dog (a much leggier type than we have today), the White English Terrier, and the Dalmatian furnished the basic crosses used by Hinks, as testified to by his son. It is quite probable that the Greyhound, Spanish Pointer, and Foxhound were also used. We do know that even in the 1930s, a Bull Terrier with a typical Hound ear would occasionally be whelped. There is some slight evidence that perhaps either the Borzoi or a smooth-coated Collie was used to help get length of head and a greater arc to the profile, for occasionally a Bull Terrier will be whelped whose head has a long, narrow muzzle that suggests a cross. (In England, cross-breds can be registered and in four generations are classed as purebreds.)

The Bull Terrier Ch. Tarquin, imported to the United States in 1880. With him is the Dalmatian "Captain".

25

As an example of the difficulty of tracing any of the early pedigrees with any degree of accuracy, in the Kennel Club *Stud Book* for 1874 there are no less than a dozen Bull Terriers with the name of Hinks' famous sire, Madman.

In these very early days, classes were generally divided above or below 16 pounds and some of the early Standards go as low as five pounds. Sometime in the 1880s, a middle-weight class was established, so that the division became: under 20 lbs., 20 lbs. to 30 lbs., and over 30 lbs. Of this division, Vero Shaw wrote in *The Illustrated Book of the Dog* (1890):

> The institution of a class for middle-weights by the Committee of the Kennel Club has practically destroyed the old Bull Terrier. At the time the innovation was suggested we remonstrated most strongly with the perpetual president of the club—Mr. Shirley, himself a Bull Terrier breeder—against the scheme. We pointed out to him that if persisted in, the change would degrade the breed, by rendering it too easy to breed a good dog, as the main difficulties were to get first-rate heavy weights and first-rate little ones. . . . The appeal was ineffectual, the result being that now a good dog of 45 lbs. is indeed a *rara avis* and the 16 pounder is extinct.

Bull Terrier Clubs

Various attempts were made in England to start a Bull Terrier Club, but it was not until 1888 that efforts were successful and The Bull Terrier Club was formed. The Colored Bull Terrier Club was formed in 1937.

In the United States, the Bull Terrier Club of America made application for active membership in the American Kennel Club on July 19, 1895. The name was submitted and approved at the American Kennel Club meeting November 12, 1895, making it the forty-seventh Club to be admitted to active membership. (There were also a number of associate members of the AKC at that time.)

This date of 1895 conflicts with the erroneous date of 1897 generally used in the Club's records. Frank F. Dole was the first president of the Bull Terrier Club of America, J.P.D. Brereton the first secretary, and Arthur Thomson was the first delegate.

A dog became a champion during that era when he had won three prizes in a challenge class, and the *Gazette* listed all living

The Bull Terrier, Count (by Marquis ex Kit), whelped January 1882. Imported to America in 1885 by Frank F. Dole.

White Wonder and Sherborne Queen, whelped about 1890. Breeder, W. J. Pegg.

Eng. Ch. Bloomsbury King, whelped 1898, cropped after winning his championship. Bred and owned by H. E. Monk. King's type was pretty much the ideal in the United States until the 1930s.

champions in each issue. (At the time the Bull Terrier Club of America joined the American Kennel Club, 1895, there were twelve living Bull Terrier champions.) The challenge class was confined to dogs that had won four first prizes in the open class at recognized shows, one of which shows had to offer at least $1,750 in cash prizes.

Two of the top dogs of the time were Ch. Streatham Monarch and Ch. Carney. These two dogs met for the first time in Chicago at the four-day Mascoutah Kennel Club Show. The judge, Harvey L. Goodman, stated in his critique that "The open class for dogs over 30 lbs. was the sensation of the show, as it was here that Streatham Monarch and Carney met for the first time on this side of the water. . . . Ultimately I placed them equal first. In doing so I well recognized Monarch's grand head, strong, powerful jaw, well-set eye and expression, also his great bone and good feet. But aside from these points, Carney excels. He beat his rival in color of eye, cleanness of neck, compactness of body, coat and carriage of stern."

The English ban on cropping, 1895, set the breed back considerably. It came about as the result of a letter that King Edward VII wrote to the Kennel Club, as its patron, in which he strongly expressed his opinion that cropping must stop. It was equivalent to a royal command, and so cropping was stopped.

At first, any type of erect or semi-erect ear was permissible. Gradually, the present type ear developed, but even now the exact shape and placing of the ear on the head is by no means standardized. Some modern ears are small and narrow with little lobe, and are placed near the top of the head. Others are large and wide with ample lobe, and placed on the side of the head. Dogs with the latter type ear tend to be or to grow coarse and are not to be favored.

In the United States, no official action was taken against the cropped ear until late 1956, when the new Standard specified an erect ear. Cropped ears had been called for by the Standard until the early thirties, but the Standard was then changed to permit of either a cropped or an uncropped ear.

When back in 1896 The American Kennel Club proposed a rule to prohibit cropping. Bull Terrier fanciers waxed so hot over the subject that the Bull Terrier Club of America was first suspended and later expelled from membership in the AKC. The Bull Terrier Club of America was dropped from the list of clubs in the May 18, 1897, issue of the *American Kennel Gazette*.

Apparently there was then a considerable reorganization of the Club because an application for reinstatement was received on July 20th and Arthur Thomson (the delegate of the exiled Club) was elected delegate and approved by the American Kennel Club in December 1897.

The AKC never did take any action against cropping. It was not until 1928 that an uncropped Bull Terrier—Blodwen of Woenwood—became a champion.

I can find no record as to when the Bull Terrier Breeders Association was started, but apparently it was around the turn of the century. There was evidently quite a duplication of membership with the Bull Terrier Club of America. At one time there was a Western Division of the Association. In 1911 the Western Division was dropped from the American Kennel Club rolls, having tendered its resignation in 1909.

About 1930 there was a "Bull Terrier Club of the West," of which John Sinnot was president. The Chicago Bull Terrier Breeders Association was started about that time. In 1931 came two new specialty clubs—the Bull Terrier Club of Ohio, with James Berner as president, and the Bull Terrier Club of Cincinnati, with DeWitt T. Balch as president. The Bull Terrier Club of New York was also started about that time. Later in the thirties came the Knicker-bocker Bull Terrier Club, also of New York, the Pacific Coast Bull Terrier Club, and then the Bull Terrier Club of California. Other sectional Clubs active at this time were the Bull Terrier Club of Cincinnati, Midwest States Bull Terrier Association, and the Cleveland Bull Terrier Club. All of these clubs went out of exist-ence before 1946.

In Canada there were the Bull Terrier Club of Canada, the Nova Scotian Bull Terrier Club, and the Bull Terrier Club of the Maritimes—all now defunct. There is now a Bull Terrier Club of Ontario and a renewed interest in the breed, all the happier in that the Bull Terrier was once the national dog of Canada.

The Bull Terrier Club of Philadelphia was reorganized in 1926, but there is no accurate record of the original Club. In 1931 the Bull Terrier Club of New England was organized with 40 members, and Mrs. Drury L. Sheraton (secretary-treasurer of the Bull Terrier Club of America) was elected president. Both of these Clubs are still in existence. In 1928 the Golden State Bull Terrier Club was started and after a somewhat checkered career became the most outstanding sectional Bull Terrier Club ever to have been formed in the United States. Today its specialty shows generally have a larger entry than do those of the Bull Terrier Club of America, and its membership is larger than that of the parent organization.

Other regional Bull Terrier clubs in the United States today include the Pittsburgh Bull Terrier Club, the Fort Dearborn Bull Terrier Club (organized in 1964, with 35 at the first meeting), the Midwest Bull Terrier Club (1965) and the Miniature Bull Terrier Club (1966).

There was a sound reason for the growth of the sectional clubs during the thirties, an influence which resulted in eighty Bull Terriers being benched at Westminster in 1930 and continual talk of a goal of one hundred. This was discussed by the late Enno Meyer, then treasurer of the Bull Terrier Club of Ohio, who wrote in the Bull Terrier column in the *American Kennel Gazette:*

> I think it is a good plan for each section of the country to develop the prevailing families in each district, and then breed to those that are similarly line-bred in other sections. This is what the Bull Terrier Club of Ohio has in mind. At a recent meeting, Willard Bitzer presiding, we compared pedigrees and agreed to exchange services and help one another in every way. In fact, you might say that we are pooling our dogs with the intention of producing something outstanding. It does not matter who may own the dog, we will all feel that we have had a part in its production and will all be as pleased as if each one was the fortunate owner.

This desire to progress as a breed, rather than as a collection of individuals each going his own way, brought about a desire to investigate and learn, as indicated in an article by Benno Stein in the *Gazette.* He states,

> All specialty clubs should seriously consider changing their Standards so as to prohibit ear cropping. But before this step is undertaken much educational work would have to be done. Such work cannot be done in two months. It would take several years perhaps.
>
> In September, 1931, the American Kennel Club ruling only prohibited the showing of dogs with cropped ears in the United States where any cropping laws were on the books, but did not change Standards of the breed affected.
>
> It should be remembered that in order to breed a certain type of ear, possibly it will be necessary to make other changes in the dog. For instance, after years of breeding, fanciers may find out that they can get a certain type of ear only by changing the whole head of the dog.
>
> To my knowledge very little research work of any kind has been made as to what kind of ears would be desired in the breeds affected by the proposed law. Take Great Danes and Doberman Pinschers as examples. It hardly seems possible that fanciers of these breeds would decide on ears carried erect, as it would take too many years before it would be possible to breed erect ears on these breeds However, it is to be feared that all breeds where a standing ear is out of the question may decide on the next best thing in that direction; that is, a small ear. I said it is to be feared because the popular trend seems to be to breed full ears without seriously considering other qualifications.

This association of physical qualities is a fascinating one and there is much of interest to be found in Dr. Leon F. Whitney's *The Basis of Breeding*, (now unfortunately out of print), especially the chapter on "Character Association." For example, as the result of experiments, Dr. Whitney came to the conclusion that the length of a dog's ear may have something to do with his scenting ability—i.e., the longer the dog's ear, the better his scenting ability.

The exact shape of ear desired for a Bull Terrier has not yet been set in any Standard. Probably majority agreement would be that the ear should be well up towards the top of the skull, small and narrow, with a minimum of lobe—coming rather close in appearance to the effect created by the old-fashioned properly cropped ear.

The first Specialty show held by the Bull Terrier Club of America of which I have been able to find record was held in Philadelphia on November 26 and 27, 1908. There were 56 entries with eight absentees, and the judge was W. Freeland Kendrick, later mayor of Philadelphia. Devil's Deputy, owned by Martin and Green, was the Winners' Dog and Merry Widow, same owners, was Winners' Bitch.

Classes then were entirely different from what they are now. In some of the classes, both sexes were shown together—puppy dogs and bitches over six and under nine months; puppy dogs, nine to twelve months; yearling dogs twelve to twenty-four months; green dogs (never before shown); novice dogs; undergraduate dogs (never having won a first); limit dogs under 30 lbs.; limit dogs over 30 lbs.; non-champion dogs; special class (never having won a first in winners' class); champion dogs; American-bred or Canadian-bred dogs; dogs bred by exhibitor; open dogs and bitches under 30 lbs.; open dogs and bitches over 30 lbs.

In 1908 the modern regular classes were established—puppy, novice, limit, American-bred, and open. (The limit class gave way to bred by exhibitor in 1950.) The old graduate class was replaced by the American-bred. Any other classes such as green, junior, etc., were no longer considered as regular classes and had to be judged after the winners' class.

At that time, breeds were generally divided into two classes— large dogs and small dogs. Bull Terriers were classed as among the small dogs.

In 1909 the new American Kennel Club rules stated that "The classification at all shows must be arranged and published in the premium lists and catalogs in the following order:

Large-sized dogs: Bloodhounds, St. Bernards, Great Danes, Russian Wolfhounds, etc.

Medium-sized dogs: the Bull Terrier, Pointers, Setters, Dachshunds, Cocker Spaniels, Poodles, Dalmatians, Airedales, etc.

Small-sized dogs: French Bull Dogs, Boston Terriers, Fox Terriers, Irish Terriers, Scottish Terriers, White English Terriers, Chinese Crested Dogs, etc.

Cage Dogs: Pomeranians, Pekingese, Pugs, Maltese, Chihuahuas, etc.

In addition, the new rule stated "Special prizes can be classified and judged on the following division of breeds: Sporting Division (which included Bull Terriers) and Non-Sporting." The Sporting Division included most of what are today's Terriers, excluding Skye Terriers.

In 1910 the American Kennel Club ruled that no longer could judges use a catalog for the judging and that the Judge's Book must be used instead.

About that time, shows were assigned points according to the total number of dogs entered. Specialty clubs that were members of the American Kennel Club automatically were entitled to four-point shows if they complied with the rules.

In 1916 the *Stud Book* was closed to all American-bred dogs whose sires and dams had not previously been registered. Not until 1932 did all puppies have to be registered as a litter. In 1954 the present "Litter Kit" was introduced so that the breeder receives a "kit" with a page for each dog in the litter: he merely fills out supplementary information when he sells or registers a dog. These steps made it progressively more difficult to falsify records.

In 1916 the first all-Terrier show was held on the roof of the McAlpin Hotel in New York.

In 1925, the *Gazette* began to publish record of top wins such as Bests in Show and Groups. Before that there was, so far as I have been able to find out, no nationally printed record of such top wins. Therefore, prior to 1925 it is impossible to check the number of times a breed may have gone Best in Show except in such a well-publicized case as that of Ch. Haymarket Faultless, who went Best in Show at Westminster in 1918.

And in 1926 appeared the *Gazette* feature that at last began to make possible a running record of the different breeds—the breed columns in the *Gazette*. Before that, any such information had been most sketchy. The first Bull Terrier column was published in the issue of July 1928, with Fred W. Ford as the author and with Ch. Haymarket Faultless as the headpiece. Ford wrote the column for several months, and then there was none until Mrs. Drury L. Sheraton took up the job with the July 1929 issue.

By this time the pattern of registration and show procedure, as well as breed Standards, had been pretty well set. Miniatures and Toys had completely disappeared from the United States, and in England the Miniature Variety was tottering, awaiting the revival that was to come in 1938, and which will be discussed in another chapter.

In 1926 came the only dog show ever put on by the American Kennel Club itself—at the Philadelphia Sesqui-Centennial Exposition. This was a three day show with 2,153 dogs in 2,899 entries; 1,767 dogs were actually benched.

The Exposition itself offered a solid gold medal for the best of each breed; on one side was a replica of the Liberty Bell and on the other side was a facsimile of the head of the Bull Terrier Ch. Queensbury Boswain. The AKC offered a solid gold medal for winners' dog and winners' bitch, and a sterling silver medal for the reserves. There were, of course, other notable prizes and over $20,000 was paid out in prize money. Even the English Kennel Club came across with an antique silver cup for Best in Show.

Alfred Delmont judged the Bull Terriers, 42 dogs with 59 entries. Winners' Dog and Best of Breed was Coolridge Prince (by Ch. Coolridge Grit of Blighty out of Coolridge Ladybird), owned by E. Koons and bred by Wyatt T. Mayer. Winners' Bitch was Newcoin Creation (by Ch. Newcoin Regret out of Newcoin Sally), owned by Frank P. Leach and bred by I. Smith. Prize money was $20 for first, $10 for second, and $5 for third in all classes. William L. Kendrick, active today as an all-rounder, offered a silver trophy for the Best American-bred Bitch, champions barred, and there were a number of other trophies and cash prizes. Indeed, it was quite a show.

The Terrier Group was judged by Alfred Delmont, Russell H.

Official seal of the Bull Terrier Club of America.
The headstudy is of Ch. Queensbury Boswain.

Johnson, Jr., and Theodore Offerman. The cash prizes in each Group were $50 for first, $30 for second, and $20 for third, plus other cash prizes and trophies. In the Terrier Group, Hon. W. Freeland Kendrick, mayor of Philadelphia and a prominent Bull Terrier breeder, offered a silver trophy for first.

The leadership of the Bull Terrier Club of England seems to have been most progressive and to have been working for the benefit of the breed as a whole. Two interesting pledges appeared in the application for membership in this club. For some time the club's constitution had forbidden the exhibiting of deaf dogs. Now it became a condition of membership that no deaf dog be bred from, that it not be exhibited, and that the applicant cooperate with the club in preventing others from so doing.

The other pledge, adopted later, was: "All members do solemnly pledge not to allow their photographs of Bull Terriers to be touched up by the photographers." However, we still see back lines and profiles, in particular, "improved."

This second pledge is an extremely important one, meant to take dishonesty and fakery out of the photographing of dogs. Only too often, the original photograph turned out to be merely the skeleton upon which the skilled retoucher painted out all the faults of the dog and endowed him with all the virtues of the breed.

In the United States, it is taken as a matter of course that this deception be practiced. It can have extremely serious results for the breed, as a breeder studying a pedigree with the aid of photographs

What you see is not always what you get. At top is Eng. Ch. Crookes Great Boy with head and tail as near to perfection as the artist could dream them. Below, alas, is a headstudy of the same dog without the artist's help.

may assume that a dog has a straight front, a level back, great fill, and a beautiful arc to its head—just because the picture says so—and be very disappointed when the litter is whelped, as he may have doubled up on the very faults he was trying to breed out.

Acceptance of the Colored

The "big battle" of this period, after Standards were set, was fought over the Colored Bull Terrier and especially over the Color Bred White. In England, the Coloreds had been making considerable progress. In 1919, Bing Boy, a brindle and white dog bred by R. S. Sievier, was the first to win a certificate. (He was by Ch. Oaksford Gladiator, out of a brindle and white bitch Stoat, pedigree unknown.) Immediately the award was challenged, but the Kennel Club upheld the judge, Major Count V. C. Hollender. In

1931 came the first Colored champion, Lady Winifred (Typical Jim—Princess Ida), bred by W. Dockerill. And then, in 1935, came the first Colored male to win its championship, Boko's Brock (Boko's Double—Expectation) bred by Miss P. K. Timins. These first two champions were brindle and white.

The increasing success of the Coloreds caused a growing feeling on the part of the breeders of the White stock that these Colored dogs, if interbred with the Whites and their progeny then used for further breeding of White strains, would cause the White strain to degenerate by bringing in faults that it had taken years to reduce in the White strain. So fearful were the breeders of the Whites that the Bull Terrier Club put on its application for membership the following pledge, "They do also undertake not to breed from brindle-bred Whites as a foundation for a White strain, and breeders and owners of Colored Bull Terriers shall, upon selling 'brindle-bred Whites,' point out the disadvantage of having 'Colored Blood' in a 'White strain.' " (After the Club agreed in 1950 to recognize the Colored dog, this was changed to: "They do undertake on selling a White dog who has a Colored ancestor within three generations that they shall reveal this circumstance to the purchaser.") The Bull Terrier Club in 1935 assumed a sort of limited jurisdiction over the Colored dogs.

In the United States, much the same pattern as developed in England followed the introduction of the Colored Variety in 1934. In that year, R. Wallace Mollison imported the first two Coloreds, Tismans Tango, a black bitch, and Brigadier of Blighty, a brindle male. These were bred together to give the first Colored litter bred in the United States, and a black-brindle from this litter was Ch. Darkfleet's Brandywine, bought by Herbert H. Stewart. Both these breeders were among the top experts of their time. Mr. Mollison had imported Int. Ch. Faultless of Blighty (later sold to the screen star Dolores Del Rio for a reported $5,000). Mr. Stewart had bred Ch. Buccaneer, three times Best of Breed at Westminster. These two men were active in securing recognition of the Colored variety by the American Kennel Club.

The Colored Variety immediately ran head on into a storm of criticism. From England, and from the Colored supporters in the States, had come forecasts of how much the Colored dog was going to contribute to the welfare of the White dog and how it was going

First Colored champion male, Boko's Brock (Boko's Double ex Expectation), finished in 1935. Bred by Miss P. K. Timins.

to cure all the ills of the breed: no longer would there be deafness, ticked coats, blue eyes or a host of other faults. These statements immediately antagonized the breeders of the White dogs, especially when they got their first look at the highly touted imported Colored dogs which on the whole left much to be desired. (I myself saw first generation Coloreds who were deaf, ticked, or blue-eyed.) The idea that these were the dogs which it was proposed to breed with the Whites to improve the Whites made no sense to the average American breeder, who felt that such assertions insulted his intelligence. It was probably the overselling of the Colored dogs more than anything else that so incensed American breeders against the Colored.

These Colored were first exhibited in 1936 at the Westminster Kennel Club in New York City, where they were shown in the same classes as the Whites. At the next Westminster show (1937), separate classes were provided. Few American breeders could see any virtue in the Coloreds that made their debut at this show.

The Bull Terrier Club of America immediately revised its Standard to disqualify any Bull Terrier with color behind the set-on of head, a device that had been tried in England with no success. Any judge who put up a Colored over a White was immediately boycotted on the basis that he had put up a disqualified dog. Indignation was great when Herbert H. Stewart put the Colored dog Ch. Wickselme's Brock's Double to Best of Breed at the 1939 Morris and Essex show. Although at that time separate classes were provided, the two colors met for Best of Breed.

In the meantime, the Color-bred White, Rebel of Blighty, in 1936 started a terrific storm that was to involve both sides of the Atlantic. Rebel became the first Color-bred White English champion.

So stirred up were the breeders of the White Variety in England that an "Extraordinary General Meeting" of the Bull Terrier Club was called to consider barring the Color-bred White from all competition for the Club's prizes, including the Regent Trophy for which Rebel had been invited to compete. The problem was left unsolved at this meeting and before the judging for the Regent Trophy brought about a further crisis, Rebel sailed for the United States, having been bought by L. Cabot Briggs.

In 1937 the Bull Terrier Club in England decided to bar all Club trophies to the Color-bred White, and this ban stood until 1950.

Also in 1937, the Bull Terrier Club inaugurated the *White Bred Stud Book* in order to protect the purity of the White strain. All dogs registered in this *Stud Book* had no Colored blood subsequent to the early matings of James Hinks and others of that day. When peace was finally signed in 1950 between the warring factions, the definition of a purebred White for the *White Bred Stud Book* was that laid down by the Kennel Club—three generations of white dogs in back of the dog to be registered.

When Rebel of Blighty came to the United States, he immediately became a storm center, just as he had been in England. The sea air was hardly out of his lungs before he appeared at the 1937 Westminster Kennel Club Show in New York, where he went Winners' Dog, Best of Winners, and then battled it out with the imported Pantigon of Enderly, an American champion, for top honors. Pantigon won—on his hind action, as the judge, T. W. Hogarth, later stated. I well remember the impression Rebel made on me, for he had by far the best expression I had ever seen—his slanting eyes and wicked look were something to be remembered in those days when a really good expression was a rarity.

American breeders felt, as had English breeders, that a top-flight Color-bred White like Rebel could cause untold harm to the breed by introducing the grave faults felt to be inherent at that time in the Colored strain. However, Mr. Briggs did not allow the dog to be used at stud with any Whites. At that stage of the development of the Colored, which needed to keep on tapping the White strain in order to breed true, this feeling probably had much basis in fact.

In 1939 the Canadian Kennel Club recognized the Colored Bull Terrier as a separate breed, which meant that litters from White and Colored parents could not be registered. This action of the Canadian Kennel Club fanned anew the hopes of the agitating members of the Bull Terrier Club of America, which immediately passed motions intended to bar registration and exhibition of Colored Bull Terriers and Color-bred Whites. The American Kennel Club gave no cooperation and so this part of the battle was quickly lost. Some years later Canada decided to handle the two varieties separately as was done in the United States, but later combined them, thus following the lead of England.

In this same year, 1939, a clause was inserted in the Constitution of the Bull Terrier Club of America stating that "It shall be deemed prejudicial to the best interests of the Club if a member breeds a Colored and White Bull Terrier or the progeny of such a

Ch. Ormandy
Dancing Time

40

Eng. & Am. Ch.
Rebel of Blighty

union." This provided grounds for the expulsion of any member conducting such a breeding.

Wallace Mollison, one of the two sponsors of the Colored Variety in the States, and his wife immediately resigned. Other resignations followed, for some of the most canny breeders had become interested in the Coloreds.

In England, prior to 1950, the Bull Terrier Club several times had found itself in an uncomfortable position due to its having banned Color-bred Whites from competition for club trophies. Color-bred Whites were qualifying for club trophies, and second-place dogs were being awarded them. The skill of some of the breeders of Coloreds had produced several outstanding Color-bred Whites. It came to be recognized that these breeders were going to outstrip the breeders of Whites as they were able to tap the fruits of White progress, whereas the breeders of Whites were unable to take advantage of the progress which the Coloreds were obviously making. The situation had changed decidedly from the thirties. Raymond Oppenheimer, the leading breeder of the day, announced that if he found a Color-bred White that would help the breed progress, he would have no hesitancy in breeding to it—and he later did exactly that with his famous, undefeated Ch. Ormandy Dancing Time.

So in 1950 the hatchet was buried and the battle in England was over. Mr. Douglas Lindsay and Mrs. G. M. Adlam took the lead in a

Eng. & Am. Ch. Dulac Heathland's Commander, whelped 1954, Best in Show all-breeds the first time shown in America. Commander achieved 8 Bests in Show and in 1957 became the first Colored to win over the Whites at the Specialty. He was the Isis Vabo Trophy winner for 1957. Owned by Dr. E. S. Montgomery.

movement to put both the White and the Colored on an equal basis in all respects. All barriers on interbreeding were removed, and all club trophies became open to all. Where trophies had been restricted by their donors to the purebred White, it was voted to accept the Kennel Club definition of a purebred dog, e.g., one whose parents, grandparents and great grandparents were all White (even though the great grandparent might have Colored brothers or sisters).

This decision of the Bull Terrier Club was a milestone in the progress of the breed. Almost immediately there was an improvement in the quality of the White dogs, especially in their head qualities. Now the White breeders could tap such a great source of heads and bone as Ch. Romany Reliance.

Today there is hardly a really top dog whose excellence does not owe something to the qualities developed in the Colored strain which is part of his background. In fact, the February 1956 Open Show of the Bull Terrier Club was in itself a testimonial to the truth of the above statement, for nearly every dog or bitch competing for the Jugs and the Regent Trophy was either the child or the grandchild of Eng. Ch. Ormandy's Limpsfield Winston, the white brother of the red Eng. Ch. Romany Rhinegold.

In the United States, in 1942, the American Kennel Club very sensibly settled the "battle of the colors" by making the Colored a separate Variety. The Colored and White Varieties then were only to compete with each other in the Terrier Group.

With no further controversies to keep animosities alive, feeling towards the Colored gradually died down. In 1948, on motion of Herbert H. Stewart, the Bull Terrier Club of America voted to recognize the Colored Variety and to provide classes for them at its 1949 Specialty Show held in New York City in conjunction with the Associated Terrier Club. Four Coloreds were benched at this first show, although nine had been entered.

For the first time since 1942, Colored and White competed together again at the 1953 Specialty Show of the Bull Terrier Club of America, when the Jug offered by the Bull Terrier Club of England was offered on a hastily drawn motion which provided for the winning White and the winning Colored to compete for the Jug. The White, Am. Ch. Taverner of Tartary, imported and owned by Mrs. S. G. Yearsley, placed over the Colored, Mysterio Charmain (who later became a champion), bred and owned by Mrs. Helen A. Boland.

In 1954, the American Kennel Club ruled that at any Specialty Show not held in conjunction with an all-breed show, the White and Colored Varieties would have to meet for a Best of Breed. (At all-breed shows, the two varieties compete against each other only in the Terrier Group). Therefore at the Specialty Show held in conjunction with the Associated Terriers in February, 1957, the Colored and the White again competed against each other for a Best of Breed, under the new American Kennel Club ruling and the Colored dog, Int. Ch. Dulac Heathland's Commander, went to the top.

As may be inferred from the foregoing, the Colored Variety has had a rugged time of it in the United States, as it did in England. Interest in the Coloreds in the States has not been too widespread. Entries have generally been on the small side. The first Colored champion whelped in the United States was Beltona Brindigal, a daughter of Boko's Beltona, who had been imported in whelp by W. J. McCortney.

43

Ch. Romany Ritual, four times Best in Show in the early 1950s. Owned by Dr. Montgomery.

Ch. Slam of Blighty was imported by Mr. Stewart in the late thirties. After that, I recall no Colored importations of any importance until after 1950, when several good ones were brought over—Int. Ch. Romany Remarkable, by Percy R. Davis, and Int. Ch. Kentigern Baronswood Firefly, by Colonel James K. Marr, both of California; Ch. Baronswood Herald of Westmeath and Ch. Brendon Burntwood of Westmeath, by Mrs. Florence Gogarty; Ch. Abraxas Oldtrinity Spaniard and Ch. Romany Ritual (four times Best in Show, all breeds), by Dr. E. S. Montgomery. In 1956, Dr. Montgomery imported Eng. Ch. Dulac Heathland's Commander, who went Best in Show, all breeds, the first time shown in the States, and then again won the Terrier Group the next day.

The Bull Terrier Club of America disposed of an incubus in 1951 when it was finally able to shelve a constitution that had stifled all efforts to progress. The old constitution provided that proxies should be allowed for voting on all matters including elections, and so the gathering of proxies by one or two members could hamstring the Club. This new constitution provided that all members could vote on all matters including elections and that any member making an important motion could force a vote by the entire membership if it were necessary; proxies were eliminated.

The Club had in the past produced several "Annuals," the first being published in 1934. In 1951 an "Annual" was produced in the form of *Bull Terriers of Today,* which devoted itself to promoting a better understanding of type. Over sixty pages of advertisements

44

picturing dogs of members were contracted for, these pictures showing Bull Terriers playing together, winning Terrier Groups, going best in show all breeds, etc., in addition to the editorial illustrations. A copy was sent to every all-breed judge, to every Terrier Group judge, and to everybody else who had a license to judge Bull Terriers. The effectiveness of this may be reflected in the interesting fact that from 1951 to 1955 inclusive, more Bull Terriers in the United States won Best in Show awards than in the entire previous history of the breed, culminating in Int. Ch. Kashdowd's White Rock of Coolyn Hill setting a record for the breed of ten such wins by the end of 1955.

Until 1967, the Bull Terrier Club of America had held its annual meeting at New York in February (in timing with Westminster), but it is now held in conjunction with the Specialty in September.

The author judging Staffordshire Terriers at Westminster 1955. Until 1936, the Staffordshires were known as American Bull Terriers or Yankee Terriers.

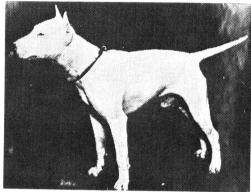

Two views of the immortal Ch. Haymarket Faultless, Best in Show all-breeds at Westminster in 1918. Owned by R. H. Elliott.

Int. Ch. Faultless of Blighty (by Rubislaw ex Broncroft Bridget), whelped 1932, pictured with some of her trophies including the painting of her by Herbert H. Stewart. Faultless, winner of two Bests in Show, was imported by F. Wallace Mollison, and later sold for a reported $5,000. to Miss Dolores Del Rio, the movie star.

3

The Show Winners

Best in Show all-breeds

The first Bull Terrier on record to go Best in Show all-breeds in the United States was the Canadian-bred Ch. Haymarket Faultless, when he topped the Westminster entry in 1918. At that time, Best in Show was judged by two men, with a third being ready to be called in as referee if necessary. Vinton Breese held out for the Bull Terrier, Charles G. Hopton held out for the Pekingese, and neither would give an inch. So George P. Thomas, the referee, was brought in and agreed with Mr. Breese that the Bull Terrier was the better dog.

I have heard that a California dog, Ch. Sound End Sombrero, went Best in Show several times before 1918, and such research as I have been able to make seems to bear this out. However, writing to the descendants of the family that owned him has brought no answer and so we will have to put this dog's wins down as a probability, but not a verified certainty.

The following is a listing of the Bull Terriers that have gone Best in Show all-breeds in the United States through the end of 1970. The parenthesized figures represent the total Bests in Show won by the dog. The d or b following the dog's name identifies whether it was a dog or bitch, and the W or Col identifies its Variety—White or Colored.

Ch. Haymarket Faultless, d-W (1)
Ch. Cloudland White Mits, b-W (1)
Ch. Cylva Barbara, b-W (2 or 3)
Int. Ch. Faultless of Blighty, b-W (2)
Ch. Ferdinand of Ormandy, d-W (1)
Ch. Heir-Apparent to Monty-Ayr, d-W (1)
Ch. Forecast of Monty-Ayr, d-W (1)
Ch. Argent Arrogance, d-W (1)
Ch. Tap Dancer of Tartary, b-W (1)
Int. Ch. Braxentra Balechin, d-W (2)
Ch. Marko of Monty-Ayr, d-W (1)
Ch. Romany Ritual, b-Col (4)
Int. Ch. Kashdowd's White Rock of Coolyn Hill, d-W (10)
Int. Ch. Dulac Heathland's Commander, d-Col (8)
Ch. Dancing Master of Monty-Ayr, d-W (10)
Ch. Radar of Monty-Ayr, d-W (6)
Ch. Rombus Andante, b-W (3)
Ch. Ormandy's Westward Ho, d-W (2)
Ch. Masterpiece of Monty-Ayr, d-W (1)
Ch. Dulac Heathland's Commander, d-Col (8)
Ch. Bathwick's Bonnie, b-Col (1)
Ch. Rombus Astronaut of Lenster, d-Col (1)
Ch. Abraxas Ace of Aces, d-Col (1)
Ch. Agates Bronzino, d-Col (1)

Int. Ch. Dulac Heathland's Commander and Int. Ch. Kashdowd's White Rock of Coolyn Hill each went Best in Show in their first time shown in the United States. Ch. Cloudland White Mist and Ch. Haymarket Faultless were Canadian-bred, the five dogs of Monty-Ayr prefix were American-bred, and all the rest were imports from England.

Eng. & Am. Ch. Kashdowd's White Rock of Coolyn Hill, Regent and Ormandy Dog Jug winner for 1953 and Isis Vabo Trophy winner 1955 and 1956. Like Int. Ch. Dulac Heathland's Commander, White Rock was Best in Show the first time shown in America. His win of ten all-breed Bests in Show stands as a record that he jointly holds with Ch. Dancing Master of Monty-Ayr. White Rock, owned by Mr. and Mrs. Z. Platt Bennett, is pictured in his win of Best of Variety at Westminster 1955. Author Ernest E. Eberhard is the judge, and Johnny Roberts the handler.

Best in Show winner Ch. Ferdinand of Ormandy, whelped 1939, by Ch. Ormandy's Mr. McGuffin ex Ch. Bedran Snow White. Pictured with his owner, Mrs. Mabie.

Ch. Forecast of Monty-Ayr, left, Best White and Ch. Madame Pompadour of Ernicor, right, Best Opposite at the 1949 Westminster. Forecast, an all-breed Best in Show winner, was the Isis Vabo Trophy winner for 1947, and "Pompy" for 1949.

Ch. Tap Dancer of Tartary, whelped 1951, Best in Show in California.

Ch. Heir Apparent to Monty-Ayr, whelped 1942, first American-bred Bull Terrier to go Best in Show all-breeds. Isis Vabo Trophy winner for 1944, 1945, and 1946.

Ch. Marko of Monty-Ayr, a Best in Show winner of the 1950s, bred and owned by Dr. E. S. Montgomery. Judge, E. D. McQuown. Handler, William Snebold.

51

Ch. Dancing Master of Monty-Ayr, American-bred appropriately whelped on July 4, 1958, winner of ten all-breed Bests in Show—a record for the breed shared with Eng. & Am. Ch. Kashdowd's White Rock of Coolyn Hill. Dancing Master is here seen handled by his breeder-owner, Dr. E. S. Montgomery, whose Monty-Ayr prefix has loomed so importantly in the Bull Terrier scene.

Ch. Radar of Monty-Ayr, whelped 1957.

Ch. Radar, an American-bred heavyweight, established an all-time record of 333 Best of Variety wins, and scored 6 Bests in Show, 45 Group Firsts and 171 Group placements. His wins included sprees of 4 Terrier Groups and 2 Bests in Show within four days, and 11 Group Firsts within ten weeks. Isis Vabo Trophy winner for 1961, 1962 and 1963. Bred by Dr. E. S. Montgomery and owned by Dr. Howard R. Doble.

Ch. Ormandy's Westward Ho, twice Best in Show. Dam of four champions in her first litter. By Ormandy Souperlative Bar Sinister ex Ch. Ormandy Duncannon Double Two. Bred by Raymond Oppenheimer, and owned by Alex T. Shaner.

Ch. Ormandy's Westward Ho, whelped 1957.

Best in Show winning father, Ch. Abraxas Ace of Aces, whelped 1965, by Eng. Ch. Ormandy's Ben of Highthorpe ex Abraxas Alvina. Isis Vabo Trophy, 1968. Bred by Miss V. Drummond-Dick and owned by Ralph Bowles.

California Best in Show winner, Ch. Argent Arrogance.

Best in Show winning son, Ch. Agates Bronzino, whelped 1967, by Ch. Abraxas Ace of Aces ex Agate's Lotus Elite. Bred by Mrs. M. O. Sweeten, and owned by Ralph Bowles and Charles Fleming. Specialty winner and Isis Vabo Trophy, 1969.

54

Ch. Rombus Andante, whelped 1961, by Eng. Ch. Souperlative Brinhead ex Ch. Romany Rosemullion, scoring one of her three Bests in Show, at Philadelphia 1963. Judge, Hollis Wilson. Owner-handler, James F. Lewis. Presenting the trophy is William L. Kendrick, the Philadelphia club president. Mr. Kendrick, now an all-breed judge, was closely identified with Bull Terrier interests in the 1920s and 1930s ("Queensbury" prefix), as was his uncle, W. Freeland Kendrick, former mayor of Philadelphia.

Ch. Kashdowd Bounce, Best White Bull Terrier at the Bull Terrier Club of America Specialty held with Ox Ridge show in 1969 under judge Alva Rosenberg (pictured), and again in 1970 under a record entry judged by Raymond Oppenheimer. Also BOV at Golden State and Philadelphia Specialty shows in 1969. Owned by Mrs. M. P. Mackay-Smith.

The Specialty Winners

From 1932 through 1951, with exception of some war years, the Specialty of the Bull Terrier Club of America was held with the Associated Terrier Clubs show in New York City in February, just prior to Westminster. The annual club meeting was also held at this time, but in 1967 it was changed to coincide with the Fall Specialty.

The first Specialty held with an all-breed club was at the Plainfield Kennel Club (New Jersey) show in 1952. The pattern of holding two parent club Specialties within a year was introduced in 1953.

Ch. Comfey, Best Bull Terrier at the Specialty and Westminster in 1932.

Until 1949 the Specialty was limited to White Bull Terriers only. With the admittance of the Colored in that year, a Best of Variety White and a Best of Variety Colored were designated, but initially they did not meet in competition. As already noted in our discussion of the acceptance of the Colored, the American Kennel Club in 1954 ruled that at any Specialty Show not held in conjunction with an all-breed show, the two Varieties would have to meet for Best of Breed. The first Specialty at which this became effective was in 1957, and the Colored BOV winner, Int. Ch. Dulac Heathland's Commander, won Best of Breed.

Where the Specialty is held with an all-breed show, there can be no Best of Breed of course, since both Variety winners are eligible to be shown in the Group. In this regard, it is interesting to note that in follow-up to his Best of Variety win at the Specialty held with the Bronx County Kennel Club all-breeds show in 1956, Ch. Kashdowd's White Rock of Coolyn Hill went on to win Best in Show. And at the Specialty held with Kennel Club of Philadelphia in 1966, Ch. Killer Joe followed his Specialty BOV with win of the very strong Terrier Group.

Winners of the Bull Terrier Club of America Specialty Shows:

1932: COMFEY (Ch. Num Skull ex Queen's Orb) —*Breeder,* H. Sumner; *Owners,* Mr. and Mrs. C. E. Brooks.

1933: WHITECOAT PERFECT LADY (Ch. No Soap ex Coolridge Topsy) — *Breeder-Owner,* H. M. Atwood.

Ch. Buccaneer, Best of Breed at Westminster in 1928, 1929 (over entry of 88), and 1930. Owned by Herbert H. Stewart.

Int. Ch. Tything Tidbit of Snug Harbor, whelped in 1931. Imported to USA by Daniel J. Bowen. Best in Specialty 1935.

Ch. Coolyn Buckskin, Best White at 1950 Specialty, Isis Vabo Trophy winner for 1950, 1951 and 1952. Bred and owned by Mr. and Mrs. Z. Platt Bennett.

58

1934: CH. FAULTLESS OF BLIGHTY (Rubislaw ex Broncroft Bridget) — *Breeder*, T. E. Davies; *Owner*, R. W. Mollison.

1935: CH. TYTHING TITBIT OF SNUG HARBOR (Gladiator's Trigo ex Tything Shure Girl) —*Breeder*, Mrs. E. T. Ingles; *Owner*, D. J. Bowen.

1936: CH. COOLYN QUICKSILVER (Ch. Coolyn Bailfire ex Ch. Brendon Bluestocking) —*Breeder*, Z. Platt Bennett; *Owner*, Mrs. Bennett.

1937: CH. COOLYN SILVERSPOT (ch. Coolyn Bailfire ex Ch. Brendon Bluestocking) —*Breeder-Owner*, Z. Platt Bennett.

1938: CH. CORSAIR MEMORY (White Memory ex Corsair Maid) —*Breeder-Owner*, J. H. Irwin.

1939: CH. COOLYN NORTHWIND (Ch. Coolyn Bailfire ex Coolyn Cavatina) —*Breeder-Owners*, Mr. and Mrs. Z. Platt Bennett.

1940: CH. COOLYN NORTHWIND.

1941: TRAMPFAST (Kowhai King Unas ex Baychuck's Dinah) —*Owner*, H. F. Stewart.

1942: RAYDIUM BRIGADIER OF COOLYN HILL (Gardenia Grandee ex Raydium Mystery) —*Breeder*, Mrs. A. Clark; *Owner*, Mrs. Z. Platt Bennett.

1943 through 1946: No Specialty.

1947: CH. RAYDIUM AVENGER OF WESTMEATH (Raydium Invincible ex Raydium White Ensign) —*Breeder*, T. J. Griffiths; *Owner*, Mrs. H. A. Gogarty.

1948: GRENADIER (Ch. Raydium Brigadier of Coolyn Hill ex Buxton Corvette).

1949: *BOV Colored:* BRANDYWINE SPITFIRE.
    BOV White: CH. COOLYN WONDER SON O' WHIRLWIND (Coolyn Whirlwind ex Coolyn Candlelight) —*Breeder-Owners*, Mr. and Mrs. Z. Platt Bennett.

1950: *BOV Colored:* CH. BARONSWOOD HERALD OF WESTMEATH (Vizor Ormandy's Loud Noise ex Baronswood Fluer-de-Lys) —*Breeder*, Mrs. E. F. Struch; *Owner*, Mrs. H. A. Gogarty.
    BOV White: CH. COOLYN BUCKSKIN (Ch. Coolyn Clipper ex Coolyn Miss Molesworth) —*Breeder-Owners*, Mr. and Mrs. Z. Platt Bennett.

1951: *BOV Colored:* CH. BARONSWOOD HERALD OF WESTMEATH
    BOV White: REGSMATH'S CONNIE GIRL (Ch. Forecast of Monty-Ayr ex Regsmath's Beautiful Girl) —*Breeder*, Constance Kermath; *Owner*, J. J. Kermath.

1952: Held with Plainfield Kennel Club all-breeds show:
    BOV Colored: CH. ABRAXAS OLDTRINITY SPANIARD (Romany Reliance ex Brendon Limpsfield Laura) —*Breeder*, Mr. and Mrs. W. Yarnold; *Owner*, Dr. E. S. Montgomery.

BOV White: CH. MARKO OF MONTY-AYR (Ch. Abraxas Oldtrinity Spaniard ex Chandra of Monty-Ayr) —*Breeder-Owner,* Dr. E. S. Montgomery.

1953: Held with Associated Terrier Clubs show:
BOV Colored: MYSTERO CHARMIAN (Ch. Baronswood Herald of Westmeath ex Coolyn Bright Penny) —*Breeder,* James A. Boland; *Owner,* Helen A. Boland.
BOV White: CH. TAVERNER OF TARTARY (Gundulph's Tower ex Sylveston Seraphin) —*Breeder,* F. Jopson; *Owner,* Coolyn Hill Kennels.

1953: Fall Specialty, held with Westchester KC all-breeds show:
BOV Colored: WESTMEATH'S BIG TOP (Ch. Brendon Burntwood of Westmeath ex Abraxas Balu of Birjand-Westmeath) —*Breeder,* Mrs. H. A. Gogarty; *Owner,* Mrs. C. J. Eldridge.
BOV White: CH. TAVERNER OF TARTARY.

1954: Held with Associated Terrier Clubs show:
BOV Colored: MONTY-AYR ABBY (Ch. Abraxas Oldtrinity Spaniard ex Ch. Blonde Bombshell of Monty-Ayr) —*Breeder,* Dr. E. S. Montgomery; *Owner,* Mrs. J. F. Cameron.
BOV White: INT. CH. BRAXENTRA BALECHIN (Ch. Ormandy's Sylveston Starshine ex Braxentra Abraxas Amelia) —*Breeder,* B. T. Traco; *Owner,* C. Hall.

1954: Fall Specialty, held with Westchester KC all-breeds show:
BOV Colored: HADES DARK TARTARUS (Ch. Sir Percival of Westmeath ex Hades Dark Princess) —*Breeder-Owner,* Hades Kennels.
BOV White: CH. REGSMATH DASHER
Breeder-Owner, J. J. Kermath.

1955: Held with KC of Philadelphia all-breeds show:
BOV Colored: CH. ABRAXAS OLDTRINITY SPANIARD
BOV White: INT. CH. KASHDOWD'S WHITE ROCK OF COOLYN HILL (Ch. Rickmay Risingstar ex Rickmay Rosina) —*Breeder,* Mrs. B. Higgs; *Owner,* Mrs. Z. Platt Bennett.

1956: Held with Bronx County KC all-breeds show:
BOV Colored: RED FIRE OF CAMALOCH (Ch. Abraxas Oldtrinity Spaniard ex Nabob Barbary Maid) —*Breeder-Owner,* Mr. and Mrs. James F. Cameron.
BOV Write: INT. CH. KASHDOWD'S WHITE ROCK OF COOLYN HILL.

1957: Held with Associated Terrier Clubs show:
BOV Colored and Best of Breed: INT. CH. DULAC HEATHLAND'S COMMANDER (Dulac Reaper of Ghabar ex Dulac Barn Owl) — *Owner,* Dr. E. S. Montgomery.
BOV White: CH. THE SPHINX OF MONTY-AYR (Ch. Marko of Monty-Ayr ex Chandra of Monty-Ayr) —*Breeder-Owner,* Dr. E. S. Montgomery.

60

Ch. Dreadnought's Mr. Panda, whelped 1965. BOV at 1967, 1968 and 1969 Specialty shows of the Bull Terrier Club of America. Owned by Dr. Leon S. Sohn.

Ch. Regsmath Dasher, Best White at 1954 Bull Terrier Club of America Specialty. Bred and owned by J. J. Kermath, former club president.

Ch. Carlings Solitaire, Best White at Bull Terrier Club of America Specialty 1969. Bred and owned by Mr. and Mrs. Carl Ackerman.

61

1958: Held with Associated Terrier Clubs show:
BOV White and Best of Breed: CH. THE SPHINX OF MONTY-AYR.
BOV Colored: CH. BATHWICK BONNIE (Ch. Phidgity Debonair of
Lenster ex Bathwick Bonne Bouche) —*Breeder,* J. F. Lipscomb; *Owner,*
Bonnyleigh Kennels.

1959: Held with National Capital KC all-breed show:
BOV Colored: CH. RED FIRE OF CAMALOCH.
BOV White: DANCING MASTER OF MONTY-AYR (Vanguard of
Monty-Ayr ex Ch. Moon Mood of Monty-Ayr) —*Breeder-Owner,* Dr.
E. S. Montgomery.

1960: Held with Sewickley Valley Kennel Club all-breeds show:
BOV Colored: CH. RED FIRE OF CAMALOCH.
BOV White: WHITE CAVALIER OF MONTY-AYR (Ch. The Sphinx
of Monty-Ayr ex Dulac Kearby's Jennie Wren) —*Breeder-Owner,* Dr.
E. S. Montgomery.

1961: Held with Westchester KC all-breeds show:
BOV Colored: CAPRICE OF MONTY-AYR (Ch. The Sphinx of Monty-
Ayr ex Dulac Kearby's Jennie Wren) —*Breeder-Owner,* Dr. E. S. Mont-
gomery.
BOV White: CH. RADAR OF MONTY-AYR (Ch. Snow Vision of Monty-
Ayr ex Ch. Snow White of Monty-Ayr) —*Breeder,* Dr. E. S. Montgomery;
Owner, Dr. Howard R. Doble.

1962: Held with KC of Philadelphia all-breed show:
BOV Colored: CH. DULAC COCK OF THE ROCK (Beechhouse Snow
Vision ex Dulac Barn Owl) —*Breeder,* Mrs. E. S. Montgomery; *Owner,*
Mrs. B. MacLeod.
BOV White: CH. DULAC BLENDED OF KEARBY (Fingalian Fiery
Cross ex Kilsae White Queen) —*Breeder,* J. Caruthers; *Owners,* Mr. and
Mrs. Wm. W. Colket.

1963: Held with Kittaning KC all-breeds show:
BOV Colored: COMMANDER OF MONTY-AYR (Ch. Dancing Master
of Monty-Ayr ex Caprice of Monty-Ayr) —*Breeder,* Dr. E. S. Mont-
gomery.
BOV White: CH. HIGHBURN ANANDEL (Fingalian Fiery Cross ex
Kilson White Queen) —*Breeder,* J. Caruthers; *Owners,* Mr. and Mrs.
Wm. W. Colket.

1964: Held with Ox Ridge KC all-breed show:
BOV Colored: HOLCROFT BLOSSOM HARRISON (Krackton Robin
of Wentwood ex Ch. Holcroft Blossom) —*Breeder,* A. Bibby.
BOV White: GOLDFINGER (Ormandy's Ben of Highthorpe ex Val-
kyrie's White Clown) —*Breeders,* R. H. Oppenheimer and E. M.
Weatherill; *Owner,* David C. Merriam.

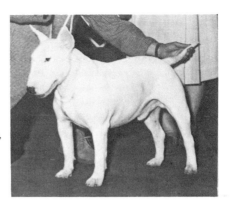

Ch. Bramblemere Duble Truble, 1966 Bull Terrier Club of America Specialty winner. Owner, Dr. Leon S. Sohn.

Ch. Goldfinger, BOV at 1964 Bull Terrier Club of America Specialty. Son of Eng. Ch. Ormandy's Ben of Highthorpe. Owner, David C. Merriam.

Ch. Swainhouse Sportsman, BOV at Bull Terrier Club of America Specialty, 1967 and 1968. Owner, Charles Meller.

63

1965: Held with Harrisburg KC all-breed show:
BOV Colored: CH. ROMBUS ASTRONAUT OF LENSTER (Souperlative Brinhead ex Romany Rosemullion) —*Breeder,* Mrs. F. E. West; *Owner,* Mrs. W. L. Heckmann.

BOV White: ORMANDY'S WESTWARD HO (Ormandy's Souperlative Bar Sinister ex Ormandy's Duncannon Doubletwo) —*Breeders,* R. H. Oppenheimer and Miss E. M. Weatherill; *Owner,* A. T. Shaner.

1966: Held with Associated Terrier Clubs show:
BOV White and Best of Breed: CH. BRAMBLEMERE DUBLE TRUBLE (Oldlane Swainhouse Superfine ex Wilsmere Alice) —*Breeder,* J. Nuttall; *Owner,* Dr. L. S. Sohn.

BOV Colored: CRESSWOOD LORD DERBY (Dulac Buff Rock ex Miss I.Q. of Monty-Ayr, C.D.) —*Breeder-Owner,* Mrs. Wm. R. Cress.

1966: Held with KC of Philadelphia all-breed show:
BOV Colored: DREADNOUGHT'S MR. PANDA (Krackton Kwait ex Lady Priscilla of Dreadnought) —*Breeder,* Betty Strickland; *Owner,* Dr. L. S. Sohn.

BOV White: KILLER JOE (Ch. Krackton Robin of Wentwood ex Holcroft Kowhai Lottie) —*Breeder-Owners,* Peggy and Michael A. Arnaud.

1967: Held with Ox Ridge KC all-breeds show:
BOV Colored: CH. DREADNOUGHT'S MR. PANDA.

BOV White: CH. SWAINHOUSE SPORTSMAN (Souperlative Masta Plasta of Ormandy ex Swainhouse Willow Wren) —*Breeder,* W. Peace; *Owner,* Charles and Susan Meller.

1968: Held with International KC of Chicago all-breed show:
BOV Colored: CH. THE SWINGER OF HY-LO (Ch. Conamor's Hooligan of Hi-Lo ex Night Star of Hi-Lo) —*Breeder-Owner,* Laura J. Campbell.

BOV White: CH. SWAINHOUSE SPORTSMAN.

1968: Held with Ox Ridge KC all-breeds show.
BOV Colored: CH. DREADNOUGHT'S MR. PANDA.

BOV White: SILVERWOOD FIRE BELLE CLAPPER (Ormandy's Thunderflash ex Silverwood Sturdee Romancy) —*Breeders,* Mr. and Mrs. Wm. W. Colket; *Owner,* Thos. B. Simmons.

1969: Held with International KC of Chicago all-breeds show:
BOV Colored: CH. AGATES BRONZINO (Ch. Abraxas Ace of Aces ex Agates Lotus Elite) —*Breeder,* Mrs. M. O. Sweeten; *Owners,* Ralph Bowles and Charles A. Fleming.

BOV White: CARLINGS SOLITAIRE (Ch. Holcroft Diplomat ex Pollyanna of Monty-Ayr) —*Breeder-Owners,* Carl and Ingrid Ackerman.

1969: Held with Ox Ridge KC all-breeds show:
BOV Colored: CH. CARLINGS MINNIE THE MASHER (Franda's Brandysnap ex Pollyanna of Monty-Ayr) —*Breeder-Owners,* Carl and Ingrid Ackerman.

BOV White: CH. KASHDOWD BOUNCE (Romany Rover Scout ex Valkyrie Gemini) —*Breeders,* Mrs. J. Higgs and W. Jarrett; *Owner,* Mrs. W. Mackay-Smith.

1970: Held with International KC of Chicago all-breeds show:
BOV Colored: CH. CARLINGS MINNIE THE MASHER.
BOV White: TRES PETITE OF MELROSE (Ch. Killer Joe ex Melrose's Salute to Ernicor) —*Breeders,* D. K. Rose and Bill Brake; *Owner,* Douglas K. Rose.

1970: Held with Ox Ridge KC all-breeds show:
BOV Colored: MIDNIGHT MELODY (Ch. Abraxas Ace of Aces ex Snowlady) —*Breeder-Owner,* Charles A. Fleming.
BOV White: CH. KASHDOWD BOUNCE.

Ch. Harper's Huntsman. Isis Vabo Trophy winner, 1964 and 1965. Owned by T. Condon.

Ch. Wilton's Orion, son of Ch. Harper's Huntsman, winner of 3 Groups in the 1960s. Owner, Lt. Col. and Mrs. W. R. Barnes.

65

4

The Trophy Winners

TROPHIES offered by the Bull Terrier Club in England have been many and have done much to sustain interest in the breed, as they have been well publicized.

The first important such trophy was the Regent Trophy, offered by Dr. G. M. Vevers. Each year, the Committee of the Bull Terrier Club selects the dogs to compete, selection being made from among the dogs or bitches first shown the year preceding the actual selection at the Open Show of the Bull Terrier Club, usually in February. The judging is done by a panel of three, selected from the Committee of the Bull Terrier Club. It is as a memento of this win that the replica of the original bronze model, in Royal Nymphenburg porcelain, is awarded.

A trophy for the Best of Opposite Sex to the Regent Trophy winner was offered by the Golden State Bull Terrier Club, beginning in 1953.

The Ormandy Jugs are offered for competition within the sex. That is, there is one Jug to be competed for by dogs only, and one for competition by bitches only. Competitors are selected by a committee of three from among the best dogs and bitches of the past year exhibited at championship shows. Since 1957 selection has

Ch. Ormandy Souperlative Chunky, whelped 1958, Best in Show in England. Regent Trophy, 1960. Owners, R. H. Oppenheimer and Miss E. M. Weatherill.

Eng. Ch. Romany Robin Goodfellow, made history by going Best in Show all-breeds at Windsor. 1957 Ormandy Jug winner. Breeders, Miss Montague Johnstone and Miss N. Williams.

Comanche of Upend, only the third Bull Terrier to go Best in Show at an all-breed championship show in England, winning at Blackpool 1969 under Percy Roberts. Bred by Mrs. B. Butler, Comanche was imported to America in 1970 by Charles and Susan Meller and quickly made his championship.

automatically included all those who have completed their championship during the preceding year. The actual selection from among these competitors is made by a different committee of three. An inscribed plaque is given as a memento of the win. A contestant defeated one year may be invited to compete the next year.

We hear much about the "Junior Warrant." This is awarded to a dog winning 25 points, as follows: Every first prize that a dog wins counts three points if it is in a championship show, and one point if it is not.

In the United States, there used to be quite a few trophies, some of them being awarded for wins over a five year period. Perpetual trophies have largely died out, as The American Kennel Club will not approve them any more.

The principal trophies still being offered for Bull Terriers, because they were in effect prior to the ban, are the Nathaniel F. Emmons Trophy, offered in his memory (he had been secretary-treasurer of the Bull Terrier Club of America for a number of years) and the Isis Vabo Trophy.

The Emmons Trophy, limited to White Bull Terriers only, was first offered in 1935 at the Eastern Dog Club show in Boston, as Mr. Emmons was a Boston man. It was intended that a memento of the win be given the winner and that he should hold the Trophy itself for one year. The Trophy was to have been offered once each year at a show selected by the Bull Terrier Club of America, the intention being to rotate it between such shows as Westminster, the

Specialty Show and Morris & Essex. It was usually offered at the Specialty Show.

The Isis Vabo Trophy was first awarded in 1940 for the winner of 1939, as it was offered to the Bull Terrier going Best of Variety the most times during the year at three-point shows or better; Terrier Group placements counted the same as breed wins. The donor was L. Cabot Briggs, who also offered a memento as a remembrance of the win. The Trophy was offered in memory of Mr. Briggs' imported bitch, Isis Vabo, who had completed her English championship at the age of only seven and a half months, but who died shortly after being brought over to the United States.

A listing of the winners of the Isis Vabo trophy is included in this chapter. There is a bit of confusion about 1944; Ch. Dinah Chips tied with Ch. Heir Apparent to Monty-Ayr in point shows, but Heir Apparent won or placed in ten Terrier Groups. In 1945 and 1946, Ch. Heir Apparent to Monty-Ayr won the trophy, and Ch. Forecast of Monty-Ayr won it in 1947, but did not receive it officially.

Another coveted American trophy is the Challenge Cup offered by the Golden State Bull Terrier Club. It is awarded annually to the Bull Terrier winning the most of a selected list of shows during the year, and its competition is restricted to California shows.

In 1970, the Bull Terrier Club of America established an Annual American-Bred Competition, to be judged by two judges with a third as referee. A trophy for the winner, to be designated as The Silverwood Trophy, was offered by the Bull Terrier Club (England) in memory of Mr. and Mrs. William W. Colket.

Eng. Ch. Titania of Tartary, Regent Trophy 1952. Bred and owned by T. J. Horner.

69

The Regent Trophy, awarded for the best dog or bitch first shown at a Championship show in the year preceding the award. Winner receives a plaque, and all competitors receive a medal.

Eng. Ch. Brendon Becky, Regent Trophy 1930.

70

REGENT TROPHY WINNERS

1930   CH. BRENDON BECKY (b,w)
       (Gladiator's Trigo ex Ch. Rhoma)
       Breeder-Owner: Mrs. G. M. Adlam

1931   CH. RINGFIRE OF BLIGHTY (d,w)
       (Ch. Beshelson Bayshuck ex Ch. Debonair of Drum)
       B: P. Sharp - O: H. K. McCausland

1932   CH. GARDENIA (d,w)
       (Silver Mystery ex Lady Marjorie)
       B-O: H. W. Potter

1933   ISIS IO (b,w)
       (Rubislaw ex Broncroft Bridget)
       B: T. E. Davies - O: Mrs. E. Mallam

1934   CH. GARDENIA GUARDSMAN (d,w)
       (Silver Mystery ex Lady Marjorie)
       B-O: H. W. Potter

1935   GUARDSON OF WICKSELME (d,w)
       (Ch. Gardenia Guardsman ex Gardenia Garbo)
       B: H. W. Potter - O: Mrs. M. E. Ayris

1936   GARDENIA CLEOPATRA (b,w)
       (Ch. Gardenia Guardsman ex Gardenia Barbara)
       B-O: H. W. Potter

1937   CH. RAYDIUM BRIGADIER (d,w) - Exported to U.S.A.
       (Gardenia Grandee ex Raydium Mystery)
       B: Mrs. A. Clark - O: Mrs. G. M. Adlam

1938   CH. VELHURST VINDICATOR (d,w)
       (Velhurst Verdict ex Velhurst Villette)
       B-O: Mrs. Stephen Phillips

1939   CH. ORMANDY'S MR. McGUFFIN (d,w)
       (Ch. Krackton Kavalier ex Ch. Cedran White Queen)
       B: R. H. Oppenheimer and Mrs. R. Clifford-Turner
       O: R. H. Oppenheimer

1940 to 1946 - No awards because of the war.

1947   CH. ORMANDY'S KERTRIM BO'SUN (d,w)
       (Ch. The Knave of Ormandy ex Kertrim Charmaine)
       B: Mr. and Mrs. J. Walker - O: R. H. Oppenheimer

71

1948　PICTISH PEONY (b,c)
　　　　(Ch. Romany Reliance ex Pictish Foxglove)
　　　　B: W. Keetch - O: D. Rainy Brown

1949　WOODEN WILLIAM (d,w)
　　　　(Ch. Ormandy's Kertrim Bo'sun ex Wooden Wildflower)
　　　　B-O: Miss E. M. Woods

1950　CH. MELVIN SON OF MARGUERITE (d,w)
　　　　(Melvin Midshipman ex Melvin Marguerite)
　　　　B: W. Watkin
　　　　O: W. Watkin, G. Melville and Mrs. J. Stevenson

1951　CH. BEECHHOUSE ROAMER OF RAVENHURST (b,c)
　　　　(Abraxas Oldtrinity Spaniard ex Vizor Buhl)
　　　　B: W. J. Sayce - O: J. S. J. Swales

1952　CH. TITANIA OF TARTARY (b,w)
　　　　(Ch. Melvin Son of Marguerite ex Tranquility of Tartary)
　　　　B-O: T. J. Horner

1953　CH. KASHDOWD'S WHITE ROCK (d,w) - Exported to U.S.A.
　　　　(Ch. Rickmay's Rising Star ex Rickmay's Rosina)
　　　　B-O: B. Higgs

1954　CH. ORMANDY SOUPERLATIVE SNOWFLASH (d,w)
　　　　(Bradbourne's Prince Regent ex Souperlative Soap Bubble)
　　　　B-O: R. H. Oppenheimer and Miss E. M. Weatherill

1955　CH. ORMANDY SOUPERLATIVE SPURRELL (d,w)
　　　　(Ch. Ormandy Limpsfield Winston
　　　　 ex Souperlative Amelia Bebe)
　　　　B-O: R. H. Oppenheimer and Miss E. M. Weatherill

1956　CH. PHIDGITY SKY HIGH (d,w)
　　　　(Ch. Ormandy Souperlative Spurrell ex Phidgity Shepherdess)
　　　　B-O:　Miss L. Graham-Weall

1957　CH. SOUPERLATIVE RAINBOW (b,w)
　　　　(Ch. Phidgity Sky High ex Ch. Souperlative Summer Queen)
　　　　B-O: Miss E. M. Weatherill

1958　CH. MELTDOWN BEAUTY SPOT (b,w)
　　　　(Ch. Ormandy Souperlative Snowflash ex Souperlative Silvertan)
　　　　B-O:　Mrs. M. Treen

1959　BRAMBLEMERE GAY CAROLYNDA (b,w)
　　　　(Ch. Meltdown Moonraker ex Ch. Bramblemere Sweet Ruth)
　　　　B: Mrs. E. Ruse - O: D. Kaye

72

Eng. Ch. Guardson of Wickselme, Regent Trophy 1935.

Eng. Ch. Gardenia, Regent Trophy 1932. The Bull Terrier was higher on leg in those days. Today's dogs are lower on leg and stouter.

Eng. Ch. Velhurst Vindicator, Regent Trophy 1938.

73

1960   CH. ORMANDY SOUPERLATIVE CHUNKY (d,w)
        (Ch. Phidgity Phlasher of Lenster
         ex Ch. Souperlative Summer Queen)
        B: Miss E. M. Weatherill - O: R. H. Oppenheimer

1961   CH. ROMANY ROMANTIC VISION (d,w)
        (Ch. Romany Robin Goodfellow ex Ch. Phidgity Snow Dream)
        B: Miss L. Graham-Weall
        O: Miss Montague-Johnstone and Miss M. Williams

1962   CH. SOUPERLATIVE SILVERY MOON (b,w)
        (Ch. Romany Romantic Vision
         ex Ch. Souperlative Summer Queen)
        B: Miss E. M. Weatherill
        O: R. H. Oppenheimer and Miss E. M. Weatherill

1963   ARDEE RESOLUTE DEFENDER (d,w)
        (Ch. Ormandy Souperlative Princeling
         ex Ch. Ardee Really Desirable)
        B-O: Mrs. Riley Donovan

1964   CH. SOUPERLATIVE SEA CAPTAIN (d,w)
        (Ch. Souperlative Brinhead ex Ch. Souperlative Sunshine)
        B: Miss E. M. Weatherill - O: Mr. & Mrs. H. T. W. Davies

1965   CH. ORMANDY'S BARBELLE (b,w)
        (Ormandy Souperlative Bar Sinister ex Ch. Burson's Belinda)
        B: W. G. and P. Burford - O: Mr. & Mrs. H. T. W. Davies

1966   SOUPERLATIVE ROMINTEN RHEINGOLD (b,w)
        (Ch. Ormandy's Ben of Highthorpe ex Ch. Souperlative Sprig)
        B: Mrs. Chisnall
        O: R. H. Oppenheimer and Miss E. M. Weatherill

1967   WHITE KNIGHT OF LENSTER (d,w)
        (Ormandy Souperlative Bar Sinister ex Rombus Allegro)
        B: Miss D. Caunce - O: Mrs. Mankin & Miss L. Graham-Weall

1968   CH. TARGYT SILVER BOB OF LANGVILLE (d,w)
        (Langville Pilot Officer ex Estelle of Langville)
        B: G. S. Gratty - O: G. S. Gratty and H. Langford
        (Exported to U.S.A.)

1969   CH. TEJAYCEY BLANCO SANTA (b,w)
        (Ch. Ormandy's Archangel ex Ch. Ormandy's Corinthian Clipper)
        B-O: T. J. Cochrane

Eng. Ch. Ormandy Souperlative Spurrell, Regent Trophy 1955.

Eng. Ch. Ormandy's Barbelle, Regent Trophy 1965. Ormandy Jug for Bitches 1965.

Eng. Ch. Souperlative Rominten Rheingold, Regent Trophy and Ormandy Bitch Jug 1966.

Eng. Ch. Monkery's Mr. Frosty of Ormandy, Ormandy Dog Jug and Golden State Trophy 1966.

Eng. Ch. Abraxas Athenia, Golden State Trophy 1968.

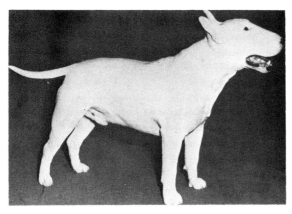

Eng. Ch. Ormandy's Caviar, Golden State Trophy 1969.

GOLDEN STATE TROPHY WINNERS
(Offered for Best of Opposite Sex to Regent Trophy Winners)

1953 CH. ORMANDY'S CHELWYN CHARLESTON (b,w)
      (Ch. Starbird of Oldparkhouse ex Vamp of Brum)
      B: Carleton Hinks
      O: R. H. Oppenheimer and T. E. Wright

1954 INGATE BLACK MAGIC (b,c)
      (Ch. Red Sky of Hardknott ex Ingate Ineffable)
      B-O: C. E. Jennings

1955 CH. PHIDGITY SNOW DREAM (b,w)
      (Ch. Ormandy Souperlative Snowflash
       ex Phidgity Shepherdess)
      B-O: Miss L. Graham-Weall

1956 DOORNTLESS GAY LADY (b,w)
      (Ch. Beechhouse Ballyhooligan ex Dauntless Melody)
      B-O: J. Thompson

1957 CH. ROMANY ROBIN GOODFELLOW (d,c)
      (Romany Golden Boy ex Ch. Romany Robinsonya)
      B: Mr. and Mrs. J. H. Robinson
      O: Miss Montague-Johnstone and Miss M. Williams

1958 ROMANY ROUGH JUSTICE (d,c)
      (Romany Recap ex Romany Rest Easy)
      B: J. Groves
      O: Miss D. Montague-Johnstone and Miss M. Williams

1959 CH. ORMANDY'S CLAYBURY MARINER (d,w)
      (Ch. Romany Robin Goodfellow ex Claybury Moneymoon)
      B: Miss V. N. Wanklyn
      O: R. H. Oppenheimer

1960 HARPER'S HEATHER GIRL (b,w)
      (Phidgity Monopoly ex Souperlative Suffragette)
      B-O: Miss D. Vick

1961 CH. ORMANDY'S DUNCANNON DOUBLE SIX (b,w)
      (Ch. Ormandy Souperlative Snowflash
       ex Ch. Claybury Moonbeam)
      B: K. Fletcher - O: R. H. Oppenheimer

1962 HARPER'S HAT TRICK OF LENSTER (d,w)
      (Ch. Gazur Phidgity Constellation
       ex Ch. Harper's Heather Girl)
      B: Miss D. Vick - O: Miss D. Vick and Mrs. Mankin

1963 CH. ROMANY ROMANTIC RITE (b,c)
      (Ch. Romany Romantic Vision ex Romany Ruderpest)
      B: Miss M. Williams
      O: Miss D. Montague-Johnstone and Miss M. Williams

1964 SOUPERLATIVE BELLA (b,w)
      (Ch. Romany Romantic Vision ex Souperlative Bittersweet)
      B: Miss E. M. Weatherill - O: P. Gwynne

1965 MELTDOWN MOONSHINER (d,w)
      (Ormandy Souperlative Bar Sinister
       ex Meltdown Princely Gift)
      B-O: Mrs. M. Treen

1966 CH. MONKERY'S MR. FROSTY OF ORMANDY (d,w)
      (Ormandy Souperlative Bar Sinister
       ex Ch. Monkery Snowflake)
      B: Mrs. P. Holmes
      O: R. H. Oppenheimer and Miss E. M. Weatherill

1967 ORMANDY'S CORINTHIAN CLIPPER (b,w)
      (Ch. Ormandy's Ben of Highthorpe
       ex Ch. Corinthian Silver Queen of Ormandy)
      B: Miss H. B. Bradbury - O: T. J. Cochrane

1968 CH. ABRAXAS ATHENIA (b,w)
      (Ch. Monkery's Mr. Frosty of Ormandy
       ex Abraxas Souperlative Viola)
      B-O: Miss V. Drummond-Dick

1969 CH. ORMANDY'S CAVIAR (d,w)
      (Ch. Ormandy's Archangel
       ex Ch. Ormandy's Corinthian Clipper)
      B: T. J. Cochrane - O: Mr. and Mrs. O. Jensen

Eng. Ch. Romany Repeat Performance, Ormandy Dog Jug 1955.

Eng. Ch. Phidgity Snow Dream
Golden State Trophy 1955.

Two Ormandy Jug winners head-on. Left, Ch. Monkery's Mr. Frosty
of Ormandy (1966 Dog) and right, Uglee Apple Blossem (1968
Bitch).

The Ormandy Jugs, presented by Raymond H. Oppenheimer to the Bull Terrier Club (England) in December 1946 as trustees for the breed. Presented to celebrate the proud record of Ch. Ormandy's Dancing Time (p. 40). The original jug, of which these are a reproduction, was presented by the Lord Mayor of London to Joseph Watte in 1666 for recovering important documents belonging to the city during the Great Fire of London.

Eng. Ch. Romany Reliance, first winner of the Ormandy Dog Jug in 1947.

ORMANDY JUG WINNERS—DOGS

1947 CH. ROMANY RELIANCE (c)
(Ormandy Sunny Day ex Romany Rivet)
B: Miss Montague-Johnstone - O: C. E. Jennings

1948 CH. ORMANDY'S EXTRA TENNER (w)
(Ch. The Knave of Ormandy ex Ormandy's Vertigo)
B: R. H. Oppenheimer - O: Mrs. L. Johnson

1949 CH. ORMANDY SYLVESTON STARSHINE (w)
(Ch. The Knave of Ormandy ex Acme of Orion)
B: Mr. and Mrs. C. E. Holland - O: R. H. Oppenheimer

1950 CH. MELVIN SON OF MARGUERITE (w)
(Melvin Midshipman ex Melvin Marguerite)
B: W. Watkin
O: W. Watkin, G. Melville, and Mrs. J. Stevenson

1951 CH. KENTIGERN RAWCLIFFE'S RADIANT (w)
(Ormandy's Top Hat of Tartary ex Tartary's Abraxas Alma)
B: Mrs. E. Ballantyne - O: D. Lindsay

1952 CH. KILSAE FOXTROT (w)
(Ch. Melvin Son of Marguerite ex Sylveston Sattalite)
B-O: Mrs. I. Simpson

1953 CH. KASHDOWD'S WHITE ROCK (w)
(Ch. Rickmay's Rising Star ex Rickmay's Rosina)
B-O: B. Higgs

1954 CH. BEECHHOUSE BALLYHOOLIGAN (w)
(Ch. The Sphinx ex Ch. Beechhouse Roamer of Ravenhurst)
B-O: J. S. J. Swales

1955 CH. ROMANY REPEAT PERFORMANCE (w)
(Ch. Beechhouse Snow Vision ex Ch. Romany Rite)
B: Miss Montague-Johnstone
O: Miss Montague-Johnstone and Miss M. Williams

1956 CH. GEORGE McRUMPUS (w)
(Ch. The Knave of Ormandy ex Oldparkhouse Moonshine)
B: Mrs. M. Aitken - O: Mrs. H. M. Allardice

1957 CH. ROMANY ROBIN GOODFELLOW (c)
(Romany Golden Boy ex Ch. Romany Robinsonya)
B: Mr. and Mrs. J. H. Robinson
O: Miss Montague-Johnstone and Miss M. Williams

81

1958   CH. ABRAXAS ACROPOLIS (w)
       (Ch. Ormandy Souperlative Snowflash
        ex Abraxas Accomplishment)
       B-O: Miss V. Drummond-Dick

1959   CH. ORMANDY'S CLAYBURY MARINER (w)
       (Ch. Romany Robin Goodfellow ex Claybury's Moneymoon)
       B: Miss V. N. Wanklyn - O: R. H. Oppenheimer

1960   CH. SOUPERLATIVE BRINHEAD (w)
       (Ch. Phidgity Phlasher of Lenster
        ex Ch. Souperlative Summer Queen)
       B: Miss E. M. Weatherill
       O: R. H. Oppenheimer and Miss E. M. Weatherill

1961   CH. ROMANY ROMANTIC VISION (w)
       (Ch. Romany Robin Goodfellow ex Ch. Phidgity Snow Dream)
       B: Miss L. Graham-Weall
       O: Miss Montague-Johnstone and Miss M. Williams

1962   CH. ORMANDY SOUPERLATIVE SPEAKEASY (w)
       (Ch. Phidgity Phlasher of Lenster
        ex Ch. Souperlative Sweet Talk)
       B: Miss E. M. Weatherill
       O: R. H. Oppenheimer and Miss E. M. Weatherill

1963   ARDEE RESOLUTE DEFENDER (w)
       (Ch. Ormandy Souperlative Princeling
        ex Ch. Ardee Really Desirable)
       B-O: Mrs. M. Riley Donovan

1964   CH. SOUPERLATIVE MASTA PLASTA OF ORMANDY (w)
       (Ch. Souperlative Brinhead ex Ch. Souperlative Sunshine)
       B: Miss E. M. Weatherill
       O: R. H. Oppenheimer and Miss E. M. Weatherill

1965   MELTDOWN MOONSHINER (w)
       (Ormandy Souperlative Bar Sinister
        ex Meltdown Princely Gift)
       B-O: Mrs. M. Treen

1966   CH. MONKERY'S MR. FROSTY OF ORMANDY (w)
       (Ormandy Souperlative Bar Sinister
        ex Ch. Monkery Snowflake)
       B: Mrs. P. Holmes
       O: R. H. Oppenheimer and Miss E. M. Weatherill

Eng. and Am. Ch. Targyt Silver Bob of Langville, Regent Trophy and Ormandy Dog Jug, 1968. Now in the United States, owned by Kenneth Neuman, he made AKC championship in four showings.

Ch. Bank Top Julius, Ormandy Dog Jug 1969.

83

1967 CH. DENSPUR'S SHEIKH (w)
      (Souperlative Acetylene ex Denspur's Sylph)
      B: R. Spurden - O: Mrs. M. Armor

1968 CH. TARGYT SILVER BOB OF LANGVILLE (w)
      (Langville Pilot Officer ex Estelle of Langville)
      B: G. S. Gratty - O: G. S. Gratty and H. Langford

1969 CH. BANK TOP JULIUS (w)
      (Ch. Romany River Pirate ex Denspur's Salome)
      B: E. Judd - O: Mrs. E. R. McQuire

ORMANDY JUG WINNERS—BITCHES

1947 CH. ORMANDY'S PENNY WISE (w)
      (Ch. The Knave of Ormandy ex Ormandy's Arabella)
      B: R. H. Oppenheimer - O: Mrs. E. Ballantyne

1948 ROSE OF HARDKNOTT (c)
      (Nightriders Temeraire ex Moonlight of Hardknott)
      B: Mrs. M. E. Bennett - O: Miss E. M. Hawthorn

1949 PICTISH PEONY (c)
      (Ch. Romany Reliance ex Pictish Foxglove)
      B: W. Keetch - O: D. Rainy Brown

1950 CH. SAX BRADBOURNE'S RHAPSODY (w)
      (Ch. The Knave of Ormandy ex Bradbourne's Model Girl)
      B: H. Jordan - O: Mrs. W. B. Marriott

1951 CH. BEECHHOUSE ROAMER OF RAVENHURST (c)
      (Abraxas Oldtrinity Spaniard ex Vizor Buhl)
      B: W. J. Sayce - O: J. S. J. Swales

1952 CH. HIGHVILLE LASSIE (c)
      (Ch. Romany Rough Weather ex Mardley Peggy)
      B: M. Crickmer - O: W. Turnbull

1953 CH. GHABAR QUEST (w)
      (Ghabar Riveredge Swell ex Brendon Bridie)
      B-O: Mr. and Mrs. R. Edmond

1954 SOUPERLATIVE SPRAY (w)
(Ch. Kashdowd's White Rock ex Souperlative Seed Pearl)
B-O: Miss E. M. Weatherill

1955 CH. MAERDY MELBA (w)
(Ch. Ormandy's Limpsfield Winston ex Maerdy Monaliza)
B-O: W. D. and J. T. Morgan

1956 CH. SOUPERLATIVE SUMMER QUEEN (w)
(Ch. Beechhouse Snow Vision
 ex Souperlative Spring Song)
B: H. Langford - O: Miss E. M. Weatherill

1957 CH. SOUPERLATIVE RAINBOW (w)
(Ch. Phidgity Sky High ex Ch. Souperlative Summer Queen)
B-O: Miss·E. M. Weatherill

1958 CH. MELTDOWN BEAUTY SPOT (w)
(Ch. Ormandy Souperlative Snowflash
 ex Souperlative Silvertan)
B-O: Mrs. M. Treen

1959 CH. ORMANDY'S LIMELIGHT OF WENTWOOD (w)
(Ch. Beechhouse Snow Vision
 ex Ch. Phidgity Flashlight of Wentwood)
B: Miss D. Price - O: R. H. Oppenheimer

1960 HARPER'S HEATHER GIRL (w)
(Phidgity Monopoly ex Souperlative Suffragette)
B-O: Miss D. Vick

1961 CH. ROMANY ROSEMULLION (c)
(Ch. Romany Robin Goodfellow ex Romany Rockaround)
B: Mrs. M. Mitchelmore - O: Mrs. F. E. West

1962 CH. SOUPERLATIVE SILVERY MOON (w)
(Ch. Romany Romantic Vision
 ex Ch. Souperlative Summer Queen)
B: Miss E. M. Weatherill
O: R. H. Oppenheimer and Miss E. M. Weatherill

1963 CH. CONTANGO CONSERVATOIRE (w)
(Ch. Phidgity Phlasher of Lenster
 ex Contango Claire-de-Lune)
B-O: Mrs. A. W. Schuster

1964 BURSON'S BENITA (w)
      (Ch. Ormandy's Ben of Highthorpe
       ex Ch. Burson's Belinda)
      B-O: W. G. and P. Burford

1965 CH. ORMANDY'S BARBELLE (w)
      (Ormandy Souperlative Bar Sinister
       ex Ch. Burson's Belinda)
      B: W. G. and P. Burford
      O: Mr. and Mrs. H. T. W. Davies

1966 SOUPERLATIVE ROMINTEN RHEINGOLD (w)
      (Ch. Ormandy's Ben of Highthorpe
       ex Ch. Souperlative Sprig)
      B: Mrs. Chisnall
      O: R. H. Oppenheimer and Miss E. M. Weatherill

1967 CH. CONTANGO CLEVER ME (w)
      (Ormandy Souperlative Bar Sinister
       ex Ch. Contango Quelle Chance)
      B-O: Mrs. A. W. Schuster

1968 UGLEE APPLE BLOSSEM (w)
      (Ch. Ormandy's Ben of Highthorpe
       ex Souperlative Cyclamen)
      B-O: Mrs. G. A. Chamberlain

1969 CH. TEJAYCEY BLANCO SANTA (w)
      (Ch. Ormandy's Archangel
       ex Ch. Ormandy's Corinthian Clipper)
      B-O: T. J. Cochrane

86

Uglee Apple Blossom, 1968
Ormandy Bitch Jug.

Ch. Contango Clever Me,
1967 Ormandy Bitch Jug.

Ch. Tejaycey Blanco Santa,
Regent Trophy and Or-
mandy Bitch Jug 1969.

87

Mrs. Drury L. Sheraton presents the Isis Vabo Trophy honoring Ch. Madame Pompadour of Ernicor in 1949.

ISIS VABO TROPHY WINNERS

1939   CH. COOLYN NORTH WIND (d,w)
       (Ch. Coolyn Bailfire ex Coolyn Cavatina)
       Breeders-Owners: Mr. and Mrs. Z. Platt Bennett

1940   CH. COOLYN NORTH WIND

1941   CH. COOLYN NORTH WIND

1942   CH. ANOTHER QUEEN OF BRUM (b,w)
       (Bing Bang of Brum ex Hockley Supreme)
       B: W. Timms - O: Mrs. George W. Mabee

1943   CH. RAYDIUM REPULSE (d,w)
       (Raydium Revenge ex Raydium Mystery)
       B: Mrs. A. Clark
       O: Mrs. H. Gogarty and B. W. Bantill

1944   CH. HEIR APPARENT TO MONTY-AYR (d,w)
       (Int. Ch. Raydium Brigadier ex Tanark Queen Mother)
       B: Dr. E. S. Montgomery - O: Mrs. E. S. Montgomery

1945   CH. HEIR APPARENT TO MONTY-AYR

1946   CH. HEIR APPARENT TO MONTY-AYR

1947   CH. FORECAST OF MONTY-AYR (d,w)
       (Ch. The Sorcerer of Monty-Ayr
        ex White Princess of Monty-Ayr)
       B-O: Dr. E. S. Montgomery

1948   Not Awarded

1949   CH. MADAME POMPADOUR OF ERNICOR (b,w)
       (Ch. Babylon Ace of Monty-Ayr
        ex Ch. Elsie Dinsmore of Ernicor)
       B-O: Ernest Eberhard

1950   CH. COOLYN BUCKSKIN (d,w)
       (Coolyn Clipper ex Coolyn Miss Molesworth)
       B-O: Mr. and Mrs. Z. Platt Bennett

1951   CH. COOLYN BUCKSKIN

1952   CH. COOLYN BUCKSKIN

1953   INT. CH. BRAXENTRA BALECHIN (d,w)
       (Ch. Ormandy's Sylveston Starshine
        ex Braxentra Abraxas)
       B: Mrs. B. T. Trow - O: Clor Myr Kennels

1954   INT. CH. BRAXENTRA BALECHIN

1955   INT. CH. KASHDOWD'S WHITE ROCK OF COOLYN HILL (d,w)
       (Ch. Rickmay's Rising Star ex Rickmay's Rosina)
       B: Mrs. B. Higgs - O: Mrs. Z. Platt Bennett

1956   INT. CH. KASHDOWD'S WHITE ROCK OF COOLYN HILL

1957   INT. CH. DULAC HEATHLAND'S COMMANDER (d,c)
       (Dulac Reaper of Ghabar ex Dulac Barn Owl)
       B: Mrs. B. MacLeod - O: Dr. E. S. Montgomery

1958 CH. SILVERWOOD TOP GRADE (d,w)
      (Eng. Ch. Beechhouse Snow Vision
       ex Warewood White Maiden)
      B: W. J. Dewhirst - O: Mr. & Mrs. W. W. Colket

1959 CH. DULAC BLENDED OF KEARBY (d,w)
      (Kearby Kihikihi ex Crescent Catamount)
      B: H. Mill - O: Mr. & Mrs. W. W. Colket

1960 CH. DULAC BLENDED OF KEARBY

1961 CH. RADAR OF MONTY-AYR (d,w)
      (Snow Vision of Monty-Ayr ex Snow White of Monty-Ayr)
      B: Dr. E. S. Montgomery - O: Dr. Howard R. Doble

1962 CH. RADAR OF MONTY-AYR

1963 CH. RADAR OF MONTY-AYR

1964 CH. HARPER'S HUNTSMAN (d,w)
      (Eng. Ch. Phidgity Phlasher of Lenster
       ex Eng. Ch. Harper's Heather Girl)
      B: Miss D. Vick - O: Thomas Condon

1965 CH. HARPER'S HUNTSMAN

1966 CH. ORMANDY'S BURSON'S BOUNTY (d,w)
      (Souperlative Sea Captain ex Burson's Benita)
      B: R. H. Oppenheimer and Miss E. M. Weatherill
      O: James F. Lewis III

1967 CH. ORMANDY'S BURSON'S BOUNTY

1968 CH. ABRAXAS ACE OF ACES (d,c)
      (Eng. Ch. Ormandy's Ben of Highthorpe
       ex Abraxas Alvina)
      B: Miss V. Drummond-Dick - O: Ralph Bowles

1969 CH. AGATES BRONZINO (d,c)
      (Ch. Abraxas Ace of Aces ex Agate's Lotus Elite)
      B: Mrs. M. O. Sweeten
      O: Ralph Bowles and Charles Fleming

Ch. Dulac Blended of Kearby, Isis Vabo Trophy 1959 and 1960. Best White at BCoA Specialty 1962. Owned by the late Mr. and Mrs. William W. Colket.

Ch. Ormandy's Burson's Bounty, Isis Vabo Trophy 1966 and 1967. Owned by James Lewis.

Ch. Silverwood Top Grade, Isis Vabo Trophy 1958. Owned by Mr. and Mrs. Colket.

Judge David C. Merriam posed between Ch. Swainhouse Sportsman (at right) and Sportsman's daughter, Ch. Conamor Joy of Hi-Lo.

5

The Bull Terrier in the
United States: 1959-1970

by David C. Merriam

IN this period of a little over a decade, the Bull Terrier has achieved greater prominence in the Terrier group and Best in Show than for many years. Although it is risky to evaluate the Bull Terrier scene by reference only to Group and Best in Show winners, they are important because they seem to set the standard for the times.

The year 1959 was dominated by the winnings of two white Monty-Ayr homebreds. Dr. Montgomery's Ch. Dancing Master of Monty-Ayr (Vanguard of Monty-Ayr ex Ch. Moon Mood of Monty-Ayr) won at least four Best in Shows, and was placed in the Group on seven occasions with six of those being Firsts. This dog not only distinguished himself in the ring, but also produced at least one Best in Show son, Ch. Masterpiece of Monty-Ayr. Dr. Howard R. Doble's Ch. Radar of Monty-Ayr (Ch. Snow Vision of Monty-Ayr ex Ch. Snow White of Monty-Ayr) was warming up for his assault on the all-time winning Bull Terrier record. In 1959, he placed in eight Groups, but was destined to push his string of Best of Variety wins to well over 300.

Ch. Mighty Moe of Monty-Ayr, Best White at Golden State Bull Terrier Specialty 1965. Owners, Lt. Col. and Mrs. J. D. Pierce.

Ch. Souperlative Spice of Hesketlane, son of Thunderflash, Best White at Philadelphia BTC Specialty 1967. Owned by Irene Mann.

Ch. Mister Ernie of Hy-Lo, Golden State Challenge Cup, 1969. Owners, Mr. and Mrs. Nigel Desmond.

Ch. Krackton Robin of Wentwood, outstanding sire of more than 20 AKC champions. Robin is a son of Ch. Romany Robin Goodfellow. Owned by Alfred T. Bibby.

94

This Colored Variety was topped by two brindle bitches. Ch. Bathwick Bonnie (Ch. Phidgity Debonair of Lenster ex Bathwick Bonne Bouche), owned by Bonnyleigh Kennels had already won a Best in Show in 1957. In 1959, she placed in 30 Groups, winning 11 of them. On the West Coast, Ch. Little Willows Mary Ann (Ch. Little Willows Young Scalp ex Pryors Prickly Pear of Tartary) easily won the Golden State Bull Terrier Club Challenge Cup and placed in three Groups. Mary Ann was owned and bred by Misses Alice and Eleanore Griffin.

The year 1959 also brought the death of Mr. Gad Root, a long-time Bull Terrier enthusiast and celebrated columnist for the breed in Dog News. Mr. Root's columns span the years 1944 to 1955 and serve as perhaps the best chronicle of the activities in the breed for those years.

The years 1960–1961 brought no new significant Bull Terriers on the show scene. Dr. Montgomery's Dancing Master continued his winning ways boosting his Best in Show total by six. At the same time, Dr. Doble's Radar increased his pace with five Bests in Show, 17 Group firsts, and 41 other Group placements.

In 1962, Jim Lewis imported the white Brinhead daughter, Rombus Andante (Eng. Ch. Souperlative Brinhead ex Romany Rosemullion). Andante scored two Bests in Show in 1962 and a spectacular Best in Show at the Philadelphia Kennel Club Show in 1963. Her win at Philadelphia created one of my favorite dog show stories. Andante had won the breed easily. Jim Lewis had stayed for the Terrier Group while several of his friends retired to the country club to await his joining them after the Group. When Andante won the group, Jim called out the good news. All celebrated. An hour or so later, Jim called out exclaiming that Andante had just gone Best in Show with Jim handling all the way! His friends suspected a bit of a put on, never imagining that a Bull Terrier would do it. To verify their doubts, they called the sports desk of the local newspaper. Being rather caught up in the dog show events, they simply asked, "Who won?" The answer came back, "Giardello." "Who is Giardello?" retorted Jim's friends. Answer: "The Boxer!" Regaling in their discovery, the exclamation came, "We knew the Bull Terrier didn't win Best in Show."

Ch. Radar of Monty-Ayr continued winning through 1962, 1963, and 1964. In total, he amassed 331 variety wins, 171 Group placements, and 51 Group firsts or Best in Shows. Clearly, the top winning Bull Terrier ever in America.

The year 1963 saw the appearance of Ch. Krackton Robin of Wentwood, imported and owned by Mr. Al Bibby, a long-time breeder under the Holcroft prefix. Robin scored two group placements in 1963, but will be recorded more significantly as a sire of importance. His brightest progeny was Ch. Killer Joe, but he also produced more champions than any other stud dog for several years in the late 1960s. Robin is a son of the great Eng. Ch. Romany Robin Goodfellow and is out of Eng. Ch. Phidgity Phlashlight, a daughter of Snow Flash.

The year 1964 found a total of 19 different Whites and seven different Coloreds placing in the Groups, although only one White, Andante, and one Colored, Ch. Rombus Astronaut of Lenster, scored Best in Show wins. Astronaut was bred by Mrs. F. E. West and was imported and shown by Mrs. Winnie Heckman. On the West Coast, Ch. Harper's Huntsman (Eng. Ch. Phidgity Phlasher of Lenster ex Eng. Ch. Harper's Heathergirl), bred by Miss Dot Vick, and imported and campaigned by Tom Condon, began making waves. During the next few years, Huntsman accumulated over 130 variety wins, with 18 Group placements including two firsts. He also won the Golden State Bull Terrier Club Challenge Cups for 1964, 1965 and 1966.

A puppy brought home from England as a gift for her husband developed into the top winning Bull Terrier for 1965. When Nancy Shaner pried loose that eleven-week-old puppy from Eva Weatherill, she little imagined that Lulu would reach for such glory. Ch. Ormandy's Westward Ho (Ormandy Souperlative Bar Sinister ex Ormandy's Duncannon Double Two) won two Bests in Show and placed in 14 Groups in 1965. This wonderfully sound and personable white bitch also distinguished herself with her first litter. Bred to Ch. Swainhouse Sportsman, she produced four champions in one litter. It is interesting to note that Lulu and Sportsman were sired by litter brothers.

Ch. Swainhouse Sportsman (Eng. Ch. Souperlative Masta Plasta ex Swainhouse Willow Wren) was imported and owned by Charles Meller. Sporty weighed a full seventy pounds at top show condition. He placed in four Groups in 1965, won several specialties in his show career, and was used extensively at stud.

Am. and Mex. Ch. Tareyton of Woodland Hills, one of the best headed California-bred dogs in . recent years. Bred by Alice Lee Willfong and owned by Darrell and Nancy Bothwell.

Ch. Vicar's Rabbit of Hy-Lo, by Ch. Abraxas Ace of Aces ex Ch. Conamor Joy of Hy-Lo, a coming together of Brinhead and Ben lines. Bred by Laura Campbell, and owned by Mr. and Mrs. Ray Williams.

Am. and Mex. Ch. Hermes' Like-able Luke, winner of the 1963 Golden State Bull Terrier Club Specialty ˙and Golden State Challenge Cup. Bred by Lynette Hamilton, and owned by David C. Merriam.

Ch. The Swinger of Hy-Lo, bitch, Best Colored at BCoA Specialty 1968 under judge Dr. Harry L. Otis. Bred and owned by Laura J. Campbell.

Another Best in Show winner in 1965 was Ch. Masterpiece of Monty-Ayr (Ch. Dancing Master of Monty Ayr ex Bonanza of Monty-Ayr) bred and shown to this win by Dr. Montgomery. Masterpiece later was owned by Jim De Mangos in California where he won. the Golden State Bull Terrier Club Challenge Cups for 1967 and 1968.

The years 1966 through 1970 brought out a number of English imports who dominated the show scene. Eng. Ch. Bramblemere Duble Truble (Oldlane Swainhouse Superfine ex Wilesmere Alice) was imported and campaigned by Dr. Leon Sohn in 1966. Jim Lewis began what would be a lengthy win streak for his Ch. Ormandy's Burson's Bounty (Eng. Ch. Souperlative Sea Captain ex Burson's Benita). Duble Truble and Bounty each won six Terrier Groups in 1966. Bounty was to extend his winning into 1967 and 1968 for a total of over 15 Group firsts.

In 1967, after a lull of several years, several Coloreds made their weight felt at the shows. Ch. Dreadnought's Mr. Panda (Krackton Kewait ex Lady Priscilla of Dreadnought) bred in America by Betty Strickland and owned and campaigned by Dr. Sohn, scored Specialty wins and topped six Groups while placing in 18 others.

The brindle and white import, Ch. Abraxas Ace of Aces (Eng. Ch. Ormandy's Ben of Highthorpe ex Abraxas Alvina) during 1967 and 1968 won one Best in Show, 21 Terrier groups and placed in 34 other Groups. He was imported by Gordon Barton for Mr. Hutchinson and was later campaigned by Ralph Bowles. Following in his father's footsteps came Ch. Agates Bronzino (Ch. Abraxas Ace of Aces ex Agates Lotus Elite) bred in England by Mrs. Sweeten. Bronzino led the field in 1969 with 7 Group firsts, 13 other placements, and several Specialty wins. In September 1970, Bronzino scored Best in Show all breeds over an entry 1,210 at Macon, Georgia. He is owned by Ralph Bowles and Charles Fleming.

In Whites, Duble Truble, Bounty, and Huntsman continued winning into 1967 and 1968. Joining them in 1967 was the home-bred Ch. Killer Joe (Ch. Krackton Robin of Wentwood ex Kowhai Lottie), bred and shown by Peggy Arnaud. Killer Joe, named after a professional dancer who was a friend of Mr. and Mrs. Arnaud, splashed into the Bull Terrier scene at the Philadelphia Specialty in 1966 where Judge Bill Colket placed him Best of Variety from the classes. In 1967 through 1969, Killer Joe won four Groups and

98

Ch. Valkyrie Milk Tray, whelped 1964, a champion before her first birthday. Owner, Mrs. Mabel H. Smith.

Like mother, like son. Ch. Robin Hood of Nottingham, by Ch. Bramblemere Duble Truble ex Ch. Valkyrie Milk Tray, also finished championship as a puppy. Breeder-owner, Mrs. Mabel H. Smith.

Abraxas Arcle, a Bar Sinister daughter. Owners, Mr. and Mrs. Wm. M. Stevenson.

placed in twelve others. He has been acclaimed by several Bull Terrier authorities as one of the best Bull Terriers ever bred in America.

On the West Coast, the brindle and white Ch. Harpers Holdfast (Starline of Lenster ex Harpers Hyacinth) bred by Miss Dot Vick and campaigned by Mrs. Boyes and Dr. Gerald Felando, won the Golden State Bull Terrier Club Challenge Cup for 1968 and 1969 and placed in over 16 Groups.

The breed was saddened in 1969 by the tragic deaths of Bill and Hope Colket. The Colkets were owners of the Silverwood Kennels in West Chester, Pennsylvania. Bill served as President of the Bull Terrier Club of America and was a frequent judge of the breed. Hope, a gentle lady and wise counselor of the breed, was the columnist for the Bull Terrier column in the American Kennel Club Gazette for several years.

The years 1969 and 1970 also noted the importation of two renowned English Bull Terriers. Eng. and Amer. Ch. Target Sylver Bob of Langville (Langville Pilot officer ex Estelle of Langville) was the 1969 winner of both the Regent Trophy and the Ormandy Jug. He was imported by Mr. Kenneth Neuman. Mr. and Mrs. Charles Meller, of Vista, California, brought over Eng. Ch. Commanche of Upend (Langville Pilot Officer ex Ch. Ormandy's Counsul Charm). Commanche made his mark in England with a smashing Best in Show at Blackpool 1969 over 4,634 dogs. Percy Roberts was the Best in Show judge.

The year 1970 was a most eventful one for Bull Terrier fanciers. For one, the eminent Raymond Oppenheimer judged the annual Specialty (held with the Ox Ridge Kennel Club show) and attracted an entry of 116 (104 dogs), an American record and a tribute to the high esteem in which Mr. Oppenheimer is held. The BOV White was Ch. Kashdowd Bounce (repeating her 1969 win), owned by Mrs. W. Mackay-Smith. BOS White was Ch. Maerdy Moonstone, owned by Mr. and Mrs. Gordon Smith. The BOV Colored, scoring in her very first show, was Midnight Melody, bred and owned by Charles Fleming. BOS Colored was Ali Baba of High Knolls, bred and owned by J. J. B. Jones.

Also in 1970 came the inauguration of the Best American-Bred Bull Terrier competition. For many years, Bill and Hope Colket

100

Ch. Killer Joe, first winner of the Silverwood Trophy given for Best American-Bred in national competition 1970. Owned by Peggy and Michael Arnaud.

had discussed with Raymond Oppenheimer the possibility of having in the United States an award equivalent to the Regent Trophy in England. It was not until after their tragic deaths that the award came to be. Appropriately, the trophy for the Best American-Bred Bull Terrier was donated by The Bull Terrier Club (England) and is designated The Silverwood Trophy. It is a wood replica of the Regent Trophy. The Bull Terrier Club also donated a trophy for the Best Opposite to the Best American-Bred Bull Terrier, designated as the Brigadier Trophy. It is a porcelain replica of the Regent Trophy which was won by Ch. Raydium Brigadier and had been willed to the club by the late Mrs. Adlam.

Instrumental in establishing the first Best American-Bred Bull Terrier Competition were BTCA president Oliver Ford and vice-president Douglas Rose. Eligibility was restricted to dogs bred and whelped in America. Following regional competition throughout the United States, the finalists came together at Old Greenwich,

Connecticut on September 20, 1970, the day after the record-establishing Specialty.

There were two judges (James Boland and David Merriam), and where they could not agree, a referee (Cecil Mann) made the decision between the two dogs the judges were considering. The 1970 winners were:

Best Colored Dog: Highland's Big Ben (Ch. Abraxas Ace of Aces ex Ch. Kearby Maywell's Gold Dust), bred by Forrest Rose and owned by Agnes and Forrest Rose.

Best Colored Bitch and Best Colored: Midnight Melody (Ch. Abraxas Ace of Aces ex Snowlady), bred and owned by Chas. A. Fleming.

Best White Dog and Best White: Ch. Killer Joe (Ch. Krackton Robin of Wentwood ex Holcroft Kowhai Lottie), bred and owned by Mr. and Mrs. Michael Arnaud.

Best White Bitch: Belle Terre's Patience (Ch. Killer Joe ex Ch. Crestmere Bettina), bred by William Schmitz and owned by William and Nancy Schmitz.

SILVERWOOD TROPHY (*Best American-Bred Bull Terrier*): Ch. Killer Joe.

BRIGADIER TROPHY (*Best Opposite*): Midnight Melody.

Of this first Silverwood Trophy competition, Raymond Oppenheimer wrote: "The Trophy Show was a great success, and I hope a fire has been lit that will never be extinguished." Those who were present at this historic occasion were convinced that they had witnessed the commencement of a new era for the breed in America.

102

BEST IN SHOW and GROUP PLACEMENT WINS
scored by White Bull Terriers since 1959

	BIS	GR1	GR2	GR3	GR4
1959:					
Ch. Romany Repeat Performance	–	–	1	–	1
Silverwood Duke Chester	–	–	–	1	–
Starlight Duchess	–	–	–	–	1
Snow Storm of Coolyn Hill	–	–	–	–	1
Ch. Onslauts David	–	1	2	2	2
Snow White Lady	–	–	1	–	–
Ch. Clar Myrs Joker	–	–	–	–	1
Ch. Silverwood Top Grade	–	–	–	1	–
Ch. Dancing Master of Monty-Ayr ..	4	6	–	–	1
Poticas Sputnik	–	–	–	–	1
Prima Ballerina of Monty-Ayr	–	–	1	–	–
Ch. Radar of Monty-Ayr	–	–	3	3	2
Dulac Blended of Kearby	–	1	1	–	1
1960:					
Ch. Dulac Blended of Kearby	–	–	7	5	6
Ch. Dancing Master of Monty-Ayr ..	1	3	2	–	–
Ch. Snow Storm of Coolyn Hill	–	–	1	1	1
Ch. Radar of Monty-Ayr	1	5	2	8	3
Greater Ajax of Coolyn Hill	–	–	–	1	–
Snowflash of Monty-Ayr	–	–	–	1	2
Silverwood Duke Chester	–	–	–	–	1
Kowhai Beechhouse Dreadful	–	–	–	–	1
Ch. Onslauts David	–	–	–	–	1
Challenge of Monty-Ayr	–	–	–	–	1
1961:					
Ch. Radar of Monty-Ayr	4	12	17	7	4
Ch. Dulac Blended of Kearby	–	–	–	–	2
Coolyn Hill Tuffy	–	–	–	–	1
Ch. Dancing Master of Monty-Ayr ..	5	7	2	–	–
Ch. White Cavalier of Monty-Ayr ..	–	1	2	–	2
Gordons Tristan	–	–	–	–	1
Snow Beau of Monty-Ayr	–	–	–	–	1
Greater Ajax of Coolyn Hill	–	–	–	–	1
Romper Rock of Coolyn Hill	–	–	1	1	1
Ch. Challenge of Monty-Ayr	–	–	–	–	1
Onslauts Pandora	–	–	–	–	1
Ch. Sonata of Monty-Ayr	–	–	1	1	–
Ch. Highburn Anandel	–	1	–	–	–
Silverwood Prince Valiant	–	–	–	1	–

103

White Bull Terrìer Winners (continued)

	BIS	GR1	GR2	GR3	GR4
1962:					
Harveys Cook of Bayou Park	-	-	-	1	-
Ch. Radar of Monty-Ayr	1	19	16	7	8
Silverwood Little Sister	-	-	-	-	1
Ch. White Cavalier of Monty-Ayr ..	-	-	1	-	-
Ch. Dancing Master of Monty-Ayr ..	-	5	1	-	-
Ch. Rombus Andante	2	5	1	2	1
Ch. Bramblemere Gay Carolynda	-	1	1	2	-
Sheridans Brown Eyed Susan	-	-	-	-	1
White Eagle of Mingo	-	-	-	1	1
1963:					
Sheridans Brown Eyed Susan	-	2	3	1	-
Ch. Radar of Monty-Ayr	-	5	9	10	6
Lady Guinevere of Melrose	-	-	-	1	-
Ch. Rombus Andante	-	7	3	1	4
Ch. White Cavalier of Monty-Ayr ..	-	-	-	2	-
Ch. Bedfords Dauntless Beauty II .	-	-	-	1	-
Ch. Lovelands Egyptian Cavalier ..	-	-	3	-	-
Silverwood Signet	-	-	-	-	1
Ch. Drum Major of Monty-Ayr	-	-	-	1	1
Ch. Krackton Robin of Wentwood ...	-	-	-	2	-
Ch. Highburn Anandel	-	-	-	-	1
Silverwood Little Sister	-	-	-	1	-
1964:					
Ch. Radar of Monty-Ayr	-	1	1	3	2
Ch. Rombus Andante	1	1	-	-	1
Wilhelms Tory	-	-	-	1	-
Samantha of Monty-Ayr	-	-	-	-	1
Ch. Harpers Huntsman	-	-	3	-	2
Ch. Lucky Strike of Monty-Ayr	-	-	-	1	-
Sassy	-	-	-	1	-
Ardee Remarkable Destiny	-	-	-	-	2
Coolyn Hill Tuffy	-	-	-	-	1
Ch. White Diamond of Onslaut	-	-	1	3	2
Ch. Dancing Master of Monty-Ayr ..	-	-	-	1	-
Fancy Prance of Burchcrest	-	-	-	-	1
Ch. Old Ironsides of Monty-Ayr ...	-	1	-	-	-
Ch. Goldfinger	-	-	3	-	-
Lady Guinevere of Melrose	-	-	-	1	-
Painted Rose of La Mirada	-	-	-	-	1
Felix Leiter	-	-	-	1	-
Ormandy's Westward Ho	-	1	-	-	-
Ormandy's Ardee Regal Duke	-	-	1	-	-

White Bull Terrier Winners (continued)

	BIS	GR1	GR2	GR3	GR4
1965:					
Ch. Goldfinger	-	-	-	1	1
Ch. Masterpiece of Monty-Ayr	1	4	1	2	2
Ch. Ormandy',s Westward Ho	2	4	5	2	3
Ch. Wilsmere Rosilla	-	-	-	1	1
Ch. Silverwood Signet	-	-	-	2	1
Ch. Sheridans Gentleman John	-	-	-	3	2
Ch. Lord Cobbolt of Dreadnought ..	-	1	-	1	5
Ch. Swainhouse Sportsman	-	-	1	2	1
Ch. Onslauts Scaramouche	-	-	-	-	1
Fairfield Fancy of Monty-Ayr	-	-	-	-	1
Ch. Harpers Huntsman	-	-	1	4	1
Bramblemere Duble Truble	-	-	-	-	1
Majorette of Monty-Ayr	-	-	-	-	1
Ch. Pussy Galore	-	-	-	-	1
Sheridans Panda	-	-	-	-	1
Lovelands Three Bars	-	-	-	1	-
1966:					
Ch. Bramblemere Duble Truble	-	6	4	6	4
Ch. Wild is the Wind in La Mirada.	-	2	2	1	3
Ch. Harpers Huntsman	-	1	2	1	2
Ch. Lord Cobbolt of Dreadnought ..	-	2	2	3	2
Ch. Masterpiece of Monty-Ayr	-	-	2	3	1
Ch. Wilsmere Rosilla	-	-	1	-	-
Diamond Jim of Abilene	-	-	-	1	3
Souperlative Spice of Heskethane .	-	1	-	-	-
Ch. Ormandy's Westward Ho	-	1	-	1	-
Ch. Swainhouse Sportsman	-	1	1	1	2
Ch. Conamor Prix De Scaramouche ..	-	-	-	1	-
Ch. Lovelands Windy McLain	-	-	-	1	-
Ch. Ormandy's Bursons Bounty	-	6	5	2	5
Ch. Wilhelms Tory	-	-	-	-	1
1967:					
Ch. Ormandy's Bursons Bounty	-	9	16	16	10
Ch. Bramblemere Duble Truble	-	-	2	1	3
Ch. Conamor Kid of La Mirada	-	-	-	2	3
Ch. La Mirada's Happy Hooligan ...	-	-	1	-	1
Gardenia of Monty-Ayr	-	-	-	1	-
Silverwood Monkerys Caviar	-	-	1	-	-
Robin Hood of Nottingham	-	-	-	-	1
Ch. Harpers Huntsman	-	-	-	1	-
Ch. Masterpiece of Monty-Ayr	-	-	-	2	3

    - continued

White Bull Terrier Winners (continued)

	BIS	GR1	GR2	GR3	GR4
1967:					
Ch. Killer Joe	-	1	-	-	1
Sheridans Panda	-	-	-	-	1
Ch. Conamor Taylorwood Like Love	-	-	1	-	-
Ch. Swainhouse Sportsman	-	-	-	-	1
Ch. Conamor Hooligan of Hi Lo	-	-	-	-	1
Ch. Goldfinger	-	-	-	-	2
Lewisfields Ransom	-	-	-	1	2
Ch. Lord Cobbolt of Dreadnought	-	-	-	-	1
1968:					
Ch. Ormandy's Bursons Bounty	-	-	1	1	1
Ch. Conamor Kid of La Mirada	-	-	2	1	4
Ch. Killer Joe	-	3	2	2	-
White Squire of Scaramouche	-	-	-	-	1
Ch. Bramblemere Duble Truble	-	-	-	-	1
Lewisfields Ransom	-	-	1	-	1
Ch. Swainhouse Sportsman	-	-	-	-	1
Flashby of Lenster	-	-	-	1	-
Cordovas Master Plasterer	-	-	1	-	1
Putnamville Sailor	-	-	-	-	1
Barclays Algonquin Queen	-	-	-	-	2
Triple Truble of Sohnrize	-	-	1	-	-
Ch. Scaramouches Souper Sphinx	-	-	-	-	1
Ch. Conamor's Hooligan of Hi-Lo	-	-	-	-	1
1969:					
Ch. Conamor Kid of La Mirada	-	-	-	1	1
Ch. His Nibs of Brobar	-	-	-	2	1
Ch. Killer Joe	-	-	3	4	-
Dreadnought's Miss Teddi Bear	-	-	-	-	1
Ch. Kashdowd Bounce	-	-	-	-	2
Ch. Triple Truble of Sohnrize	-	-	-	3	-
Herculean Terror	-	-	-	-	1
Ch. Conamore Hooligan of Hi-Lo	-	-	1	-	-
Prince Phillip of La Mirada	-	-	1	2	-
Panda's Slasher of Sohnrize	-	-	-	-	1
Ch. Holcroft Archer	-	-	-	1	-

BEST IN SHOW and GROUP PLACEMENT WINS
scored by Colored Bull Terriers since 1959

	BIS	GR1	GR2	GR3	GR4
1959:					
Ch. Bathwick Bonnie	-	11	5	8	6
Ch. Tregony Tuba	-	-	-	-	1
Ch. Little Willows Mary Ann	-	-	1	1	1
Fantasy of Monty-Ayr	-	-	-	1	-
1960:					
Ch. Bathwick Bonnie	-	5	3	3	1
Indian Summer of Monty-Ayr	-	-	-	1	1
Brindle Chief of Mingo	-	-	-	1	1
Ch. Little Willows Mary Ann	-	-	-	1	-
1961:					
Ch. Red Fire of Camaloch	-	-	-	1	-
Golden Eagle of Camaloch	-	1	-	-	1
Ch. Brindle Chief of Mingo	-	-	1	-	-
1962:					
Sheridans Sir Winston	-	2	-	2	-
Ch. Dulac Cock of the Rock	-	-	-	1	..
Brindle Princess of Mingo	-	-	-	1	1
1963:					
Sheridans Sir Winston	-	2	-	2	1
Commander of Monty-Ayr	-	-	1	-	-
1964:					
Sheridans Sir Winston	-	-	-	-	2
Lewisfields Sterling Looie	-	-	1	1	1
Red Duke of Monty-Ayr	-	-	-	1	-
Black Pearl of Camaloch	-	-	1	-	-
Ch. Holcroft Blossom	-	-	-	1	-
Holcroft Blossom Harrison	-	-	-	1	-
Rombus Astronaut of Lenster	1	2	-	-	-
1965:					
Ch. Rombus Astronaut of Lenster .	-	3	6	2	1
Lewisfield Sterling Looie	-	-	-	-	2
Black Pearl of Camaloch	-	-	-	-	1
Phidgity De Romany	-	-	-	1	-
MacJacs Keystone	-	-	-	1	-
Bilmars Tagalong	-	-	-	-	1
Cresswood Lord Derby	-	-	-	-	1

107

Colored Bull Terrier Winners (continued)

	BIS	GR1	GR2	GR3	GR4
1966:					
Ch. Rombus Astronaut of Lenster ..	-	1	1	2	2
Ch. Headmaster of La Mirada	-	-	-	-	4
Lewisfields Sterling Looie	-	-	1	1	1
Wiltons Orion	-	-	1	1	1
Old Lane Rising Son	-	1	-	-	-
Ch. Cresswood Lord Derby	-	-	-	-	1
Harpers Holdfast	-	-	-	-	1
1967:					
Old Lane Rising Son	-	2	2	2	-
Ch. Dreadnoughts Mr. Panda	-	6	7	5	6
Bejobo's Double Trouble	-	-	-	1	-
Ch. Abraxas Ace of Aces	-	12	10	3	4
Ch. Wiltons Orion	-	1	2	2	1
Ch. Headmaster of La Mirada	-	-	-	1	-
Follys Hooligan of Mackshire	-	-	-	-	1
Ch. Commander of Monty-Ayr	-	-	-	-	1
Lewisfields Sterling Looie	-	-	-	-	1
Ch. Harpers Holdfast	-	-	-	2	-
Lady Penelope of Dreadnought	-	-	-	-	1
Greystokes of Dreadnought	-	-	-	-	1
1968:					
Ch. Dreadnought's Mr. Panda	-	5	2	5	8
Ch. Abraxas Ace of Aces	1	9	6	4	7
Ch. Harpers Holdfast	-	-	5	4	6
Greystroke of Dreadnought	-	1	1	1	-
Scaramouche's Tanfastic	-	-	-	2	1
August Beauty of Monty-Ayr	-	-	-	-	1
Ch. Wilton's Orion	-	2	-	-	-
1969:					
Ch. Harpers Holdfast	-	-	-	1	-
Ch. Agates Bronzino	-	6	4	4	3
La Miradas Red Coat	-	-	2	3	2
Prince Phillip of La Mirada	-	-	1	2	-
Lewisfield's Sterling Looie	-	-	-	1	-

6

The AKC Standard
—an Introduction

THE first record we can find of a purely American standard for judging the Bull Terrier appeared in the June 30, 1915 edition of the *American Kennel Gazette,* official publication of the American Kennel Club.

However, in the October 31, 1915 issue of the *Gazette* there was published a different version of this American Standard, preceded by the explanation that "Inadvertently there was sent us by the secretary of the Bull Terrier Club of America an incorrect standard, and same appeared in the June 30, 1915 issue. We now append the correct standard as approved by the Bull Terrier Club of America."

A comparison of the two versions of this American Standard leads to the conclusion that there were differences in the thinking back of the two versions that reflected serious conflict in opinions on type. These differences were as follows:

> **First Version:** Muzzle should be neither square nor snipey, but should present a rounded appearance as viewed from above.

This seems to be obviously a different and not as clear way to define the egg-shaped head. It recalls the description of the head in the Standard of the Bull Terrier of Scotland, 1904.

Second Version: Muzzle wide and tapering, but without such taper as to make the nose appear pinched or snipey.

This type of head was contemporaneously often referred to as the "coffin-shaped" or "brick-shaped" head. It holds to the type head with a straight profile as called for by early Standards. Some prominent fanciers of the time considered that the term "down-ness" given in the Standard referred to expression, and not to any curvature of the profile. In fact, in the 1930s one breeder and judge so highly regarded the straight profile that he insisted that a Roman finish to the nose was a disqualification and judged his dogs accordingly.

The reason why this new Standard on the head was so important is that it took the development of the breed away from the direction in which it had been going, the direction being followed by English breeders. In the States, egg-shaped heads were inevitably produced, but were immediately discarded. They were not wanted as they were not considered to fit either the Standard or the fashion. The ideal head became that of Ch. Haymarket Faultless (Best in Show at Westminster 1918). A headstudy of Faultless was carried at the beginning of the Bull Terrier column in the *Gazette* until 1938, when it was replaced by a picture closer to the head type being imported by American breeders.

Another interesting difference in the two versions was the matter of weight. The first version stated "Weight is not a matter of importance, so long as a specimen is typical." The second version specified "From 12 to 60 pounds inclusive."

It is rather an astonishing thing to learn that at the time English breeders were developing the great heads and stocky bodies that were so to influence American breeders in future years, and Lord Gladiator and his descendants were setting new standards of greatness, American breeders were turning their backs on this natural evolution and breeding a type that degenerated until the English imports came on to dominate the shows in their own persons and get. It is especially astonishing when one recalls the admission of English breeders at the start of the century that more and better

Bull Terriers were to be found in America then than in all of England.

American breeders misguidedly went to great efforts to lengthen heads, which gradually weakened the muzzle and led to the oft-quoted expression "couldn't bite through a biscuit." Together with length of head was inevitably produced a leggy, narrow dog with the very characteristics that Mr. Pegg decried in the English dogs of 1907.

Around 1930, a tendency to ignore the American standard began to manifest itself. More and more dogs with uncropped ears were being shown, despite the fact that the Standard called for a cropped ear. In fact, the Bull Terrier selected for the American Kennel Club's official book of the standards, *The Complete Dog Book*, Ch. Comfey, had an uncropped ear, even though the Standard given in that very same volume (1936) called for a cropped ear.

In 1954, at the annual meeting of the Bull Terrier Club in England, it was suggested that a new Standard be drawn up. A Committee was formed, with Raymond Oppenheimer as Chairman.

In 1956, the English Standard was about complete. It was a model of simplicity and clarity. I saw the opportunity for a new American Standard and wrote Mr. Oppenheimer asking if I could copy the "new" English Standard, and he responded affirmatively. I contacted the officers of the Bull Terrier Club of America and some breeders, and all agreed it was a great idea. They felt that the English breeders who formulated the Standard had done such an excellent job that there was no need for another committee to duplicate their work, especially since a Committee of the BTCA appointed in 1952 to revise the Standard could not even agree on the head.

The new Standard was proposed and presented in its exact English form at the meeting held in July, 1956. Three changes were voted and the new Standard was approved unaminously.

The American Kennel Club unofficially stated that several changes would be necessary before the Standard could be approved. One of these changes provided for a separate Standard for each variety, rather than a combined Standard. I wrote Mr. John Neff, then Executive Vice-President of the American Kennel Club, stating that "any attempt to modernize our Standard has been met with suspicion. This is the proposed new English Standard, word for word."

111

At the regular Fall meeting of the Bull Terrier Club of America, the new Standard was voted in unaminously and adopted August 30, 1956. The American Kennel Club approved it on December 11 of the same year.

As was to be expected, there was some criticism of the new Standard. Peculiarly enough, a good part of that criticism was directed at phrases that are practically identical with those of the old Standard.

One of the outstanding features of the new Standard is that attention is concentrated upon what a dog *should be,* rather than on what it *should not be.* A judge guided by the Standard will do a better job because he knows what to look for. The judge who looks for what a dog should *not* be, will never increase his knowledge and will be constantly exposing his ignorance because he has not learned to recognize a good dog.

In eliminating a listing of faults, the Standard credits the judge with the common sense and ability, as well as the responsibility, to learn what to look for. Most of our bad judging (and bad breeding) comes from concentrating on faults rather than virtues. If the advice of those who put accent on faults were followed, the greatest Bull Terriers ever born would never have been bred.

In his column on Terriers in the October 1964 issue of *Popular Dogs,* Dr. E. S. Montgomery, famous judge and breeder (Monty-Ayr prefix), wrote:

Some years ago the Bull Terrier Club of America revised the Standard of Perfection. It then set, and still sets, a precedent and a target for *all* breed clubs. The Standard tells only what a good Bull Terrier should look like, . . . not what it should not look like.

The publication of the English Standard was delayed for three years, until 1959. It is, in general, much the same as the American.

Further revision to the American Standard was made and approved as of September 10, 1968. Two changes were made.

In the 1956 Standard, the provision for Color in the White Bull Terrier had read:

The Color should be pure white, though markings on the head are permissible. Any markings elsewhere on the coat shall disqualify.

112

This was revised to read:

The Color is white though markings on the head are permissible. Any markings elsewhere are to be severely faulted. Skin pigmentation is not to be penalized.

The 1968 Standard also made *blue eyes* a disqualification in both the White and Standard varieties.

To help the reader in his understanding of the standard, we have included diagrammed pictures illustrating some of its main points. A few words regarding the dogs used as models in these pictures may be in order.

The dog used in the profile depiction of the standard (Page 114) was, in the eyes of many highly respected authorities, one of the greatest Bull Terriers ever. In the picture his ears were caught in unfortunate position, and his tail—while correctly set on—is carried high, but in all else he well visualizes what a judge might look for in the breed.

The dog used as model in the picturizations taken straight head-on and straight from the rear was selected because of his lack of exaggeration—his points are easy to understand because his type lies between the extremes of Terrier and Bulldog. These are poses rather difficult to secure, and are not ordinarily as flattering as those taken from a slight angle. Other pictures may show dogs with a greater curvature of profile, a more exaggerated ear placement, a greater spring of rib, but none that in their entirety in the actual flesh gives such a pleasing impression of type and balance. A judge keeping this dog in mind as a modest ideal will also not go too far astray.

The skeleton has been superimposed upon the same front and rear pictures in order to better show the relationship between the actual flesh one sees and the underlying bone structure. In order to avoid the confusion of too many lines, most of which would help but little in an understanding of fundamental structure, only the principal bones have been shown.

HEAD long, strong, deep, egg-shaped; profile
should curve gently downwards from top of skull
to tip of nose

COAT short, flat, glossy, harsh
to the touch   Skin tight

EYES small, triangular,
obliquely placed

EARS small, thin,
placed close together

NOSE black,
well-developed
nostrils bent
downward at tip

NECK arched, long

BACK short, strong

LIPS clean, tight,
underjaw well-defined

TAIL, set on low,
short, thick at
base, tapering
to a fine point

STIFLE
well-bent

HOCKS
well-let-down

SHOULDERS
strong, flat

RIBS
well-rounded

CHEST deep, broad

UNDERLINE
graceful upward
curve

FORELEGS straight, big-
boned, moderate length

PASTERNS
strong, upright

FEET round,
compact,
cat-like

DISQUALIFYING FAULT:
blue eyes

7

Official Breed Standard of the Bull Terrier

*As adopted by the Bull Terrier Club of America, and
approved by the American Kennel Club, September 10, 1968.*

STANDARD FOR THE WHITE BULL TERRIER

The Bull Terrier must be strongly built, muscular, symmetrical and active, with a keen determined and intelligent expression, full of fire but of sweet disposition and amenable to discipline.

The Head should be long, strong and deep right to the end of the muzzle, but not coarse. Full face it should be oval in outline and be filled completely up, giving the impression of fullness with a surface devoid of hollows or indentations, i.e. egg-shaped. In profile it should curve gently downwards from the top of the skull to the tip of the nose. The forehead should be flat across from ear to ear. The distance from the tip of the nose to the eyes should be perceptibly greater than that from the eyes to the top of the skull. The under-jaw should be deep and well defined.

The Lips should be clean and tight.

Head, oval in outline, completely filled in, e.g. egg-like

Forehead flat across from ear to ear

Ears, erect, small, set close together

Eyes, triangular, small, obliquely placed

Shoulders strong, flat, no "heaviness"

Chest deep and broad

Forelegs of moderate length, big-boned, straight

The Teeth should meet in either a level or in a scissors bite. In the scissors bite the upper teeth should fit in front of and closely against the lower teeth, and they should be sound, strong and perfectly regular.

The Ears should be small, thin and placed close together. They should be capable of being held stiffly erect, when they should point upwards.

The Eyes should be well sunken and as dark as possible, with a piercing glint and they should be small, triangular and obliquely placed; set near together and high up on the dog's head. Blue eyes are a disqualification.

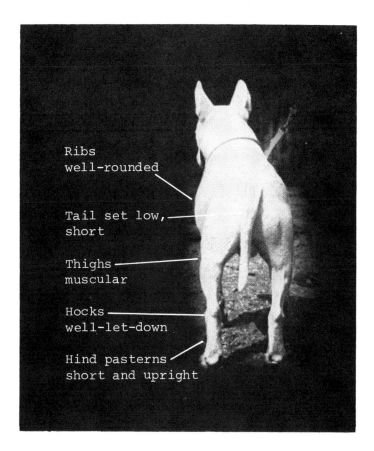

Ribs
well-rounded

Tail set low,
short

Thighs
muscular

Hocks
well-let-down

Hind pasterns
short and upright

The **Nose** should be black, with well developed nostrils bent downwards at the tip.

The **Neck** should be very muscular, long, arched and clean, tapering from the shoulders to the head and it should be free from loose skin.

The **Chest** should be broad when viewed from in front, and there should be great depth from withers to brisket, so that the latter is nearer the ground than the belly.

The **Body** should be well rounded with marked spring of rib, the back should be short and strong. The back ribs deep. Slightly arched over the loin. The shoulders should be strong and muscular but

117

without heaviness. The shoulder blades should be wide and flat and there should be a very pronounced backward slope from the bottom edge of the blade to the top edge. Behind the shoulders there should be no slackness or dip at the withers. The underline from the brisket to the belly should form a graceful upward curve.

The Legs should be big-boned, but not to the point of coarseness; the forelegs should be of moderate length, perfectly straight, and the dog must stand firmly upon them. The elbows must turn neither in nor out, and the pasterns should be strong and upright. The hind legs should be parallel viewed from behind. The thighs very muscular with hocks well let down. Hind pasterns short and upright. The stifle joint should be well bent with a well developed second thigh.

The Feet round and compact with well-arched toes like a cat.

The Tail should be short, set on low, fine, and ideally should be carried horizontally. It should be thick where it joins the body, and should taper to a fine point.

The Coat should be short, flat, harsh to the touch and with a fine gloss. The dog's skin should fit tightly.

The Color is white though markings on the head are permissible. Any markings elsewhere on the coat are to be severely faulted. Skin pigmentation is not to be penalized.

Movement. The dog shall move smoothly, covering the ground with free, easy strides, fore and hind legs should move parallel each to each when viewed from in front or behind. The forelegs reaching out well and the hind legs moving smoothly at the hip and flexing well at the stifle and hock. The dog should move compactly and in one piece but with a typical jaunty air that suggests agility and power.

Faults. Any departure from the foregoing points shall be considered a fault, and the seriousness of the fault shall be in exact proportion to its degree, *i.e.* a very crooked front is a very bad fault; a rather crooked front is a rather bad fault; and a slightly crooked front is a slight fault.

DISQUALIFICATION:
Blue eyes.

118

STANDARD FOR THE COLORED BULL TERRIER

The Standard for the Colored Variety is the same as for the White except for the sub-head "Color" which reads:

Color. Any color other than white, or any color with white markings. Preferred color, brindle. A dog which is predominantly white shall be disqualified.

DISQUALIFICATIONS:
Blue eyes.
Any dog which is predominantly white.

Eng. Ch. Romany Reliance, first winner of the Ormandy Dog Jug in 1947, one of the best heads to his time.

119

Raymond H. Oppenheimer with Ch. Ormandy
Souperlative Chunky and Ch. Burson's Belinda.

*The achievements of Mr. Oppenheimer and his
Ormandy prefix are internationally well known.
His analysis of the four varieties of Bull Terrier
type may indicate to many a breeder how he can
better his own type and go on to greater things.*

8

The Four Variations in Bull Terrier Type

by Raymond H. Oppenheimer

THERE are today four distinct types of Bull Terriers to be seen in the show ring, and a careful study of photographs of the breed back to the early days convinces me that these four types have always existed since the breed first took recognizable shape. What is more, three of these types quite clearly reveal the separate and distinct ancestry from which the Bull Terrier originated.

Many people both inside and outside the breed deplore this diversity, but I believe that keen students of Bull Terriers find in it one of the breed's greatest charms, because it admits of a considerable number of possible permutations and combinations which breeders can employ in seeking to achieve their ideal, an ideal which varies from breeder to breeder and which, in so varying, provides that spice without which any activity sinks into a dull monotony.

Let us now examine these four types and classify them, giving an outstanding modern example of each:

First, there is the Bull Terrier with the accent on "Bull," an obvious and magnificent specimen of this being Ch. Beech House Ballyhooligan.

Next, we have the Bull Terrier with the accent on "Terrier," and here we need not look further than the outstanding Ch. Kowhai Uncle Bimbo.

Third, we have the Bull Terrier with the accent equally divided between the two syllables, and a splendid example of this is Ch. The Sphinx.

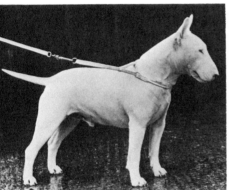 

Last, we have the "Dalmatian" type. I must make it clear that I mean no reference here to ticks. Anyone who is in doubt as to what I am trying to explain should study the photo above of the great Dalmatian Ch. Snow Leopard; if they will mentally give him a Bull Terrier's head and a pure white coat, they will see at once the similarity in build to certain famous Bull Terriers, though naturally the Bull Terriers are heavier. An obvious modern example of this type of Bull Terrier is Ch. Ormandy Souperlative Snowflash.

Three types show clearly the three breeds which were used in building up the Bull Terrier, i.e., Bulldog, English Terrier, and Dalmatian, while the fourth type is a blend of the other three.

Each of these types has it devotees, but the fascinating thing is that history teaches us—and personal experience confirms—that all four types are necessary to keep the breed progressing. A breeder who will not use the "Bulls" soon finds his line beginning to lose substance; if he will not use the "Terriers" he finds his line beginning to lack corkiness and fire; if he will not use the blended types he finds his line beginning to lack balance; while if he will not use the "Dalmatians" he is soon in trouble with a lack of reach and style.

In many books on breeding one will find the advice that it is a mistake to mate extremes together in the hope of getting something halfway between, because the puppies will normally take after one parent or the other. This advice is excellent where one is dealing with what, for want of a better expression, I will call specific physical features; e.g., it would certainly be ridiculous to mate together a dog whose feet turned out and a bitch whose feet turned in with the fantastic hope of having puppies whose feet turned neither in nor out. But where the question is one of proportions or "type," in this context, the uniting of extremes is often exceedingly successful, since the characteristics involved are ones which blend. For example, if one mates together a well-bred "Bull" and a well-bred "Dalmatian," it is distinctly exceptional to get a litter as "Bullish" or as "Dalmatianish" as either parent—and, although many geneticists will frown in displeasure at this statement, it is a demonstrable fact, and one the appreciation of which will help breeders immensely in their efforts to obtain the builds they require.

Once this fact has been understood, there is really no more one need say, since a breeder searching for a particular build has all he wants, always provided that his eye is accurate in assessing the proportions of those animals which he is examining with a view to choosing for them their mates.

As I have said earlier, some fanciers have violent personal preferences for one type or another, and the man who prefers the "Bulls" naturally finds the "Terriers" too light, the "blended types rather wishy-washy and insipid, and the "Dalmatians" too upstanding.

The man who prefers the "Terriers" finds the "Bulls" too heavy, the "blended" types unsatisfying and lacking corkiness, and the "Dalmatians" too statuesque.

The man who prefers the "blended" types finds the other three too extreme or exaggerated, while the man who prefers the "Dalmatians" finds the others lacking in reach and scope.

I am not going to attempt to say that any one type is definitely right or that any one type is definitely wrong, as it is easy to think of several outstanding animals of each type who have contributed much of benefit to the breed's progress. In fact, I believe that the hallmark of a good judge, and the greatest gift which a breeder can possess, is the ability to appreciate a good dog or bitch of any one of these types, and especially when judging I have always tried to guard against any tendency on my own part to lean towards any particular type. By this I mean that when judging, I guard against a preference for any one type—I try to concern myself only with the dog's physical perfections or imperfections. In this connection I always find the criticism, often heard at shows, that such-and-such a judge has not stuck to one type not only senseless, but also proof that the critics themselves cannot know what they are talking about, since no judge worth his salt should leave out of the reckoning a top class Bull Terrier even if it chances not to be of the type for which he has a personal predilection.

Mr. Leo Wilson once gave as his definition of a first-class judge, "a man who never puts up a bad one." I would go further and say that he must also never leave a top class dog out in the cold. For a judge to place at the top of the line a row of dogs of one particular type, some being very ordinary specimens of that type, and leave top class specimens of other types without the proverbial sausage, just because they are not his types, is in my opinion to stamp him as a bad judge. What is more, such a judge will never for long be a successful breeder.

However, I want to utter one serious word of warning. Bull Terriers can be bred so extreme in type, towards the Bulldog, or towards the Dalmatian, or towards the Terrier, as to cease to conform at all to the general type outlined by the Bull Terrier Standard, and I should not like anyone to read into what I have written a suggestion that departures of so violent a nature are good or are even to be excused by judges. The four types of which I speak are really subdivisions, within the general type, and a smooth-coated, pure white Borzoi or its opposite, a Bulldog with a Bull Terrier

125

head, should not be tolerated by any judge or breeder who knows his job.

In other words, a good judge should be prepared to assess, without prejudice, any Bull Terrier whose variation in type remains within the limits which can legitimately be said to be covered by the wording of the breed Standard. But he should equally be prepared to deal, without mercy, with any animal, however well made, which departs too far from the accepted Standard to be reasonable.

Type anywhere is and must be the prime essential of every breed, since, in the final analysis, it is only type which differentiates one breed from another or the purebred from the mongrel.

Now to pass from the general to the particular. Correct Bull Terrier type as we see it in England is a blend between the Terrier and the Bulldog, onto which is added the various specific points as set out in our Standard. A departure from that correct type towards an undue emphasis of the Terrier or Bulldog characteristics is very bad, as is any Houndy tendency, because we feel that the dog immediately ceases to conform to the basic demands of the Standard which was grounded upon the conceptions of the men who evolved the original White Bull Terrier.

I have spoken of a blend and in that connection I should make it clear that in our view, the blending not only applies to individual tendencies but also, most important of all, to the proportions. These agree proportions are not simply the outcome of the whim of some bewhiskered ancestor of the modern fancier. They are, on the contrary, based upon sound mechanical knowledge as to what best constitutes theoretically the ideal fighting machine. With that in mind, the framers of our Standard demanded width of chest for stability, shortness of back to give maneuverability and quick turning power, and enough length of foreleg for reach and agility. Onto these proportions they added the other necessary points, e.g., correct shoulders, strong hindquarters, and so on, to complete the perfect fighter.

So far so good; but there were in addition some points added on for purely aesthetic reasons (such as a white coat, no wall eyes and other points which we all know), until there emerged the picture of a splendid animal complete in every detail and of a type quite unmistakable.

126

Having said so much, I am going on to make use of something I have written elsewhere because I think it will fit into the pattern of what I have tried to say here and complete the fabric. When it was previously published it was called "A Pen Picture of a Bull Terrier" and I make no apology for repeating it with certain emendations since it sets out, as well as I can do it, what I think a Bull Terrier should look like.

Looked at full face, the head should appear long and strong and it should be oval or egg-shaped; that is to say, it should be filled up everywhere so that the surface has upon it no hollows or bumps, and there should be a minimum of loose skin, especially around the throat and mouth, while the forehead should be flat from ear to ear and not domed or peaked like a gnome. The cheeks should be flat and clean—not coarse and lumpy. The ears should be on top of the dog's head and fairly close together and should be capable of being held by the dog stiffly erect, when they should point upwards and neither sideways nor forwards. When all these features are present, the head gives a general impression of smoothness—almost as if it had been "blown up" with an air pump.

In profile the head should form nearly an unbroken line curving slowly downwards from the top almost to the end of the nose, where it should—for the last half inch or so—curve down a little more steeply, producing that feature generally referred to as the "Roman finish." Continuing in profile, the head should give an appearance of depth and should look neither shallow nor bird-like, nor should the profile to be so exaggeratedly curved or angulated as to cause the dog to look like some kind of sheep. And the head should be in proportion to the rest of the dog.

One other feature of paramount importance is the dog's eye and, more particularly, expression. The eye itself should be as nearly black as possible and it should be well sunk into the head. The opening into which the eye is sunk should be high upon the dog's head so that the distance from the nose to the eye is perceptibly greater than that from the eye to the top of the head. Further, the opening should be small, triangular, and, above all, slanting so that it points upwards and outwards. With these features the dog will have the true Bull Terrier expression which, for me, contains something of the gay, proud, mischievous, and grave, and much of the impassive, repelling, and inscrutable.

The Bull Terrier should have a wide chest with straight front legs and clean shoulders (i.e., shoulders that are not rounded or bulgy when looked at head-on). They should be firmly attached to the dog's body and the shoulder blades should be well laid back; that is to say, that a line drawn from the front and bottom of the shoulder blade to the top and back of it should point up over the middle of the dog's back and not directly upwards only just behind his head. When the shoulder blades are thus laid back, the dog's neck comes into its body in a clean sweep and not at that very unattractive near right angle which spoils so many quite nicely arched necks. A neck that is reachy, arched and muscular, and sweeps smoothly into the line of the back is one of the most distinguishing marks of a good Bull Terrier.

Looking down on the dog's back, the spring or bowing of its ribs should be plain to see and he should be much wider across his back than across his loins. Looked at sideways, the dog's brisket should be much nearer the ground than its belly; it is this formation which gives an appearance of lowness to ground as opposed to the ill-balanced, Bulldoggy, stunted appearance of so many with too short legs.

Continuing to look at the dog sideways, its back should be short, strong, and level back to the loin, where there should be a slight rise (or roach), after which the line should curve smoothly downwards and be set off nicely by the tail, which should be attached to the dog low down; it should taper from base to tip and be carried parallel to the ground. Beneath this should come well-muscled, broad hindquarters leading on downwards to a well-bent stifle and a well-angulated hock, giving almost an impression as if the dog were slightly crouched to spring. Another important attribute of a well-made dog is that the various parts of the body should be in proportion to each other. That is to say, the length of the leg should be in proportion to the width of the dog, to its length of back, and so on, and it is of paramount importance that the dog should neither be nor look disconnected.

Finally, when the dog moves, the front and hind legs should travel parallel, straight towards the observer and straight away; the dog should cover the ground easily and with a swinging, springy stride, his front legs reaching out well forward and his hind legs flexing easily at the stifle and hock, moving smoothly, truly, and

128

strongly from the hip, the dog carrying himself proudly and in one piece.

I have so far only dealt in detail with head, with make and shape, and with proportions. If to that we add big and round but not coarse bone, strong "cat" feet, a temperament obedient but full of go, and muscles rippling beneath a shining coat, we shall have gone a long way to describing a dog in which every feature is in proportion to all the others. Then the predominating impression will be not of some outstanding point, but of a general level of all-round excellence approaching the Standard's description of "a strongly built, muscular, active, symmetrical animal, with a keen determined expression, full of fire but of sweet disposition, amenable to discipline."

No one has ever bred the perfect Bull Terrier, no one ever will, but in the struggle to approach more and more nearly to the unattainable lies the source of so much happiness to so many. In the foregoing words I have tried to paint a picture of the particular unattainable which we in England are trying to approach.

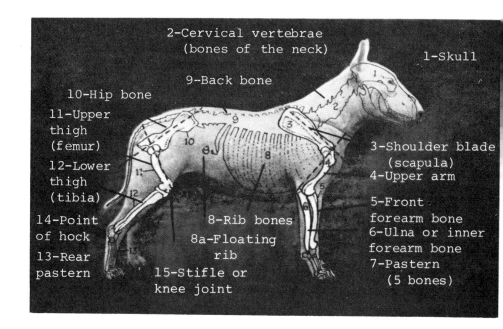

2-Cervical vertebrae (bones of the neck)

1-Skull

9-Back bone

10-Hip bone

11-Upper thigh (femur)

12-Lower thigh (tibia)

14-Point of hock

13-Rear pastern

8-Rib bones

8a-Floating rib

15-Stifle or knee joint

3-Shoulder blade (scapula)

4-Upper arm

5-Front forearm bone

6-Ulna or inner forearm bone

7-Pastern (5 bones)

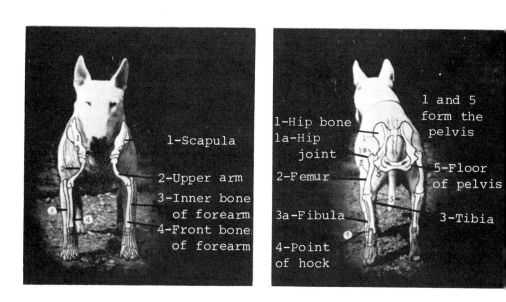

1-Scapula

2-Upper arm

3-Inner bone of forearm

4-Front bone of forearm

1-Hip bone

1a-Hip joint

2-Femur

3a-Fibula

4-Point of hock

1 and 5 form the pelvis

5-Floor of pelvis

3-Tibia

9

Skeleton of the Bull Terrier Analyzed

by T. J. Horner

> *An understanding of the main parts of the skeleton is necessary to a proper understanding of how a dog is put together under his flesh and muscle. In order to explain more fully the points depicted on the preceding two pages, it would seem a good idea to include the comments of T. J. Horner, which appeared in the 1955* Bull Terrier Club Annual, *since this is the best explanation I have seen. Today a foremost journalist and judge in England, Mr. Horner was then one of the leading Bull Terrier breeders, and his "Tartary" prefix is well known in the breed.*

ABOUT twenty years ago, Bull Terrier breeders and judges, it seems to me, were almost wholly concerned with the finishing touches to the breed—downfaces and fill-up, dark eyes, fine, tick-free coats, small neat ears, etc.; in other words, they were more concerned with the icing than the cake. It is only fair to say that in those days there were a few hardy individualists who preached make and shape, soundness and character; but theirs were voices crying in the wilderness and few heeded them, certainly not the winning owners who were content to strive for bigger and better downfaces, leaving make and shape to those cranks who were interested in it. And who can blame them? For were not the biggest winners the possessors of the best downfaces? A little before World War II there was a sudden awakening of interest in substance, and it was soon decided that a Bull Terrier could be an outstanding specimen without an outstanding head, provided it had enormous substance. Before long the cleverer breeders combined good heads and great substance, but then found that even the best Bull Terriers were still lacking in that subtle something which makes a dog look right from any angle. It was at this stage that a real interest in make and shape began to take hold of the fancy, which in a very short time has led on to the very marked improvement so apparent in the breed today.

There is nothing secret or occult about make and shape: indeed it is a fascinating subject which can be an enormous help to breeders in their efforts to produce that Perfect Bull Terrier. The skeleton is the key to make and shape, and in all normally shaped breeds is approximately the same, varying only in proportions as type varies in the different breeds.

So many people boggle at the words make and shape and turn glassy-eyed at mention of the skeleton that I think it is time to drag it out of the cupboard and take a closer look to see just how it is put together and some of the ways in which it can get out of shape. To be really successful as breeders and judges, it is essential that we should know something about the foundations on which we are trying to build our ideal. No one would try to build a house from the roof downwards, and it seems to me unreasonable to expect to breed a Bull Terrier by considering only heads and quality and leaving the rest to chance and good feeding—as so many have in the past.

The skull should have an egg-like appearance with great strength under and between the eyes. There should be a distinct downward inclination from the brow forward, but no stop; nor should there be any angle or abrupt falling away at this point. The Standard calls for an egg-shaped head—and eggs do not have angles. The under-jaw should be deep and strong and in proportion to the rest of the skull; the teeth should be level and even and fit in with their opposite numbers to give that vice-like grip so characteristic of the breed. Crooked teeth, under- and overshot jaws, weaken this grip and therefore are faults.

The neck, which is an extension of the backbone, should be long and strong enough to give the dog a proud carriage of the head and provide him with great strength and mobility in action. Too long a neck unbalances and weakens the dog, and too short a neck detracts from his mobility and gives him a stuffy appearance foreign to the breed.

The forehand consists of the shoulder blade, the upper arm, the forearm, the pasterns and the foot, and the joints which couple them together. The feet should be small, thickly padded, closely knit, and should point straight forward, standing or moving. The pasterns, which are the dog's shock-absorbers as well as providing a flexible joint between the feet and the forearm, should be short, strong, upright, and yet have a certain elasticity. The forearm with the pastern and foot forms the foreleg, which should be straight viewed from any angle, and placed well under the dog, but should not turn out nor be so closely knit to the body as to restrict movement.

The upper arm is the bone which slopes obliquely forward from the elbow to the point or base of the shoulder blade. The ideal is a long upper arm forming a right angle with long shoulder blade (when the dog is standing normally). A short upper arm leads to a steep shoulder placement, very common in our breed and often accompanied by excess muscle on shoulders, loose elbows, and .a short neck giving the animal a thick Bulldog-like appearance and very restricted action.

Shoulder blades should be long and set well back and also inclined inwards towards the withers. This formation allows of the long, arched neck, broad at the base and tapering gracefully into the skull, without loss of strength. Extremely steep shoulders are sometimes accompanied by a long neck which completely lacks arch, in extreme cases curving in towards the front of the dog. This is a ewe neck and a very ugly fault. Upright shoulders very often are accompanied by a dip behind the withers, well-laid shoulders seldom if ever are.

The chest should be broad with the brisket coming well below the elbow.

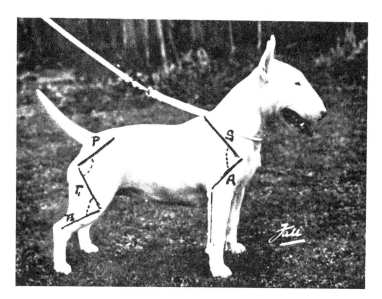

S.4   The bones angled correctly

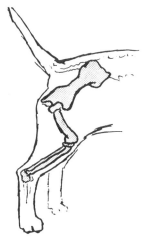

S.5   Well bent stifle

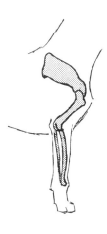

S.6   Shoulder well laid back

A study of the accompanying pictures and diagrams will show the correct angle of the bones to each other in both the fore and hind limbs. In all cases, widening the angle has a detrimental effect.

Compare the shoulder in picture S.4 with that of S.7. In S.4 the angle of the shoulder to the upper foreleg is approximately 90° which is correct. In S.7 it is wider giving the characteristic upright shoulder.

The hindquarters in S.4 and S.8 show how opening the angle gives a straight stifle joint, because the pelvis is insufficiently angled to the upper thigh.

S. —Shoulder (Scapula)

A. —Upper Foreleg

P. —Pelvis

T1. —Upper Thigh

T2. —Lower Thigh

S.F.—Stifle Joint

S.7 Upright shoulder

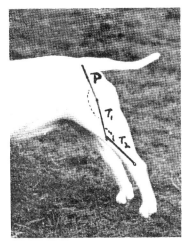

S.8 Straight stifle

135

The body of the dog is in three parts. First, the back and barrel, consisting of the section of the spine from the point of the withers to the last rib and including the ribs themselves which should be deep, well-rounded, and carried well-back. The back should be short and level and the underline of the ribs should show a graceful curve from the point of the chest up into the loins. The loins form the second part of the body and reach from the last rib to the croup—the point at which the pelvis is attached to the spine. The loins should be short, broad, and slightly arched. There should be a distinct "cut up" or rise in the under line of the belly, and the flanks should be clearly defined. Lack of these points produces a "sausage body" in which chest and belly are the same depth and chest and flanks the same thickness—a bad fault and all too common in the breed. Third, the croup, from the end of the loin to the root of the tail, should continue the arch of the loins and curve slightly downward to the tail, which should be set on low, be short, thick at the root and taper to a fine point. It should be flexible and free of breaks or kinks.

The hind legs are attached to the body by the pelvis, a large bony plate which is attached to the spine at the latter end of the loin and has at its lower extremities two ball and socket joints into which fit the upper ends of the hind legs. The hind leg consists of the femur and the tibia, the upper and lower long bones which are connected by the stifle joint. The tibia is connected to the back pastern by the hock joint and the pastern to the foot.

It is the top of the femur which fits into the socket of the pelvis at the hip, and the all-important angulation of the hind leg depends in the first place on the angle at which the pelvis is attached to the spine. The ideal—again we assume the dog to be standing normally—is halfway between vertical and horizontal, about 45° to the spine. This position permits the dog in movement to reach well forward and also allows ample drive from behind. A pelvis set at a steep angle—more nearly vertical—tends to shorten the leg bones, reduce the length of stride forward and back, and the angles at the stifle and hock giving a short choppy stilted hind action, very common in extra short-bodied dogs and usually accompanied by very steep shoulder placement—the whole giving a Bulldoggy appearance. The opposite condition when the pelvis is set at too flat an angle produces overangulation, when the dog's leg bones are unduly lengthened and the bend of stifle unduly exaggerated and the dog's hocks are pushed too far behind him, as seen in some German Shepherd Dogs. This gives a weak, uncontrolled action but is seldom seen in Bull Terriers. Even with the pelvis in the right position, unless the angles at stifle and hock are approximately correct, the dog will still be unbalanced and will be unable to move with freedom and drive. The correct angles at stifle and hock are those which in any given dog—whether he is tall or short on the leg, long or short in body—bring the stifle joints well forward under the dog, and the hocks a little further to the rear than the root of the tail. To some extent these angles are governed by the length of femur and tibia. The whole conformation of the hind legs is dependent on all the component parts being in harmonious proportion to each other so that the dog both looks and is firmly balanced on his feet and is able to move freely and strongly from his hocks. In some cases these angles are almost non-existent, giving the formation known as "straight in stifle." When the line from the hip to the foot is nearly vertical, it has the effect of pushing the dog's latter end up and gives him a dip in the back and a complete inability to move with freedom and drive.

Hocks should be well defined and remain parallel both standing and moving. The distance between them should be in proportion to the general width of the dog—they should look neither close nor wide apart. The back pasterns should be short, strong, and upright, with the hind feet rather smaller than the forefeet.

The entire skeleton should be closely knit together and the dog should move all in one piece.

No one will ever breed a quite perfect Bull Terrier, but if breeders will bear the skeleton in mind when planning matings, they will have a far better chance of achieving the impossible than if they leave it to rot in its traditional cupboard.

Herbert H. Stewart judging the 1952 Specialty Show of the Golden State Bull Terrier Club in California. Ch. Taverner of Tartary was Best of Breed and went on to win the Group. Handled by William Snebold.

Mr. Stewart was an artist and an engineer who owned Bull Terriers for close to fifty years. He was the breeder of Ch. Buccaneer, three times Best Bull Terrier at Westminster, and was internationally known as an authoritative judge who knew type thoroughly. He was among the very first to understand and appreciate the trend towards the modern type of Bull Terrier. His sketches and remarks published in Bull Terriers of Today (1951) *are so fundamental to a proper understanding of what to look for that they are reprinted here.*

138

10

Analysis of Bull Terrier Structure

by Herbert H. Stewart

SHAPE OF HEAD: The above heads are all the same length, the only difference being in downface. A1 is a poor type head, still encountered in the show ring. B1 is a much better type head, brick shaped; the top is practically straight. C1 shows a false type of downface induced by "angulation." This type head is not as powerful as D1 and is always accompanied by a high eyebrow which is a fault. It is, however, a step in the stage of evolution towards D1. D1 shows downface; this head looks shorter than A1 and B1 because fill and arc lend an optical illusion. This type head usually has a deeper, stronger underjaw which still further gives an illusion of shortness. Now to assure yourself that the drawings all show heads of the same length and proportions, measure them.

A2   B2   C2

In A2 notice how the lack of fill and the wide skull give an appearance of coarseness, whereas in C2, with the same width, the "egg-shape" gives a clean feeling despite the tremendous space for leverage where the jaw joins the skull. In B2, although the skull is clean and the expression is good, note how much weaker the head appears even though it looks to be longer.

E1   F1   G1

EYES: The eye gives the Bull Terrier its characteristic expression. E1 shows a small triangular eye that is placed as in an Airedale; there is no Bull Terrier expression here. F1 shows a deep-set round eye; again there is no Bull Terrier expression and would not be no matter how small the eye was. G1 shows an eye slanted down towards the nose—this is a true Bull Terrier eye, properly placed, and gives the true Bull Terrier expression. No matter how small, well shaped, and deep set an eye may be, it is a poor Bull Terrier eye if it is not slanted as in G1.

DOWNFACE is probably the most important development of the Bull Terrier of today. It is more than expression—it is an actual curvature of the top of the head or, as the English Standard puts it, "The profile should be almost an arc from the occiput to the tip of the nose . . . almost egg-shaped."

This "downface" is not a fad. It is the key to a stronger muzzle than the Bull Terrier ever had before. Most all powerful flesh tearing animals have downface. This gives leverage and the arrows in the sketches on this page indicate the flow lines of the power.

Note that the lobster has two claws, one long and thin for grasping like a pair of tongs, the other claw larger and thicker and used for crushing. Take a look at a Stillson wrench, the only kind that has enough leverage to unscrew a rusted pipe. Also at your own hands when they grasp something. Sort of lobster claw like, are they not?

Also note how much fill and downface there is in the head of a tiger. Then transfer this physical aspect of jaw power to the head of the Bull Terrier; see how man's selective breeding has taken this mechanical principle developed by nature and used it to give the Bull Terrier a stronger and at the same time a more beautiful head than it ever before possessed. One might almost see that "fill" and "downface" are a natural in the breed because sometimes it pops up most unexpectedly and in a big way.

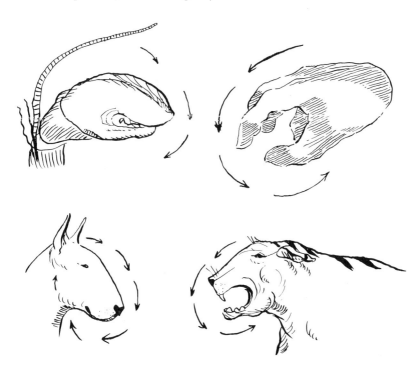

Power is the reason for the downface of the Bull Terrier, the power to grab, hold and crush as explained in the text.

BODIES are of two general types. One is short, chunky, rather low set, and compact as shown at the left. The other is long and rangy, high on leg, as shown at the right. It is obvious which gives the greater impression of power and fast action at close quarters. The rangy type may be a pretty dog, but is apt to be weedy, flat sided, with head and body too narrow. Either a straight or an angular head is likely to go with the rangy dog, whereas true down-face seems to be linked more with the chunky type.

FRONT should show straight legs, a powerful chest, clean shoulders. Again contrast the sense of power shown by the dog at the left with the narrow-chested, rangy type shown at the right. Remember that the Bull Terrier packs the most power in the least space—he should always look like a powerful, active dog, full of courage and spirit and giving the impression of having the will and the ability to meet any emergency.

REAR should be powerful. Once again see how the broad dog gives the impression of a powerful rear, whereas the rangy dog looks as if it had less power. Power without coarseness is the keynote to Bull Terrier conformation.

142

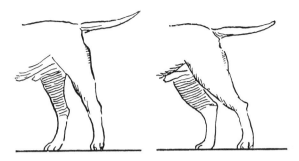

STIFLES should be well rounded and hocks well let down. Note how the high hock and straight stifle at left give an impression of weakness, whereas the rounded stifle and well-let-down hock at right give an impression of strength. Also note how the high-set tail at left looks weaker than the low-set tail at right besides contributing to a poor tail carriage.

Now let us look at the whole dog. This dog's proportions give balance. He looks game. Note that his chest is not only wide but is deep—he looks like a powerful dog able to move fast at close quarters and to turn on a dime, rather than one which would excel on the race track.

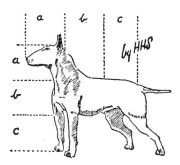

PROPORTIONS of the Bull Terrier divide themselves into three masses, and Mr. Stewart illustrates this clearly in sketches which we reprint from the 1950–51 Annual of the Bull Terrier Club of England. The text accompanying the sketches says in part, "He can be divided into three approximately equal parts. This makes the Bull Terrier head greater in proportion to his body than the heads of most other breeds, a fact which we appreciate as very important. Most artists unfamiliar with the breed, or lacking appreciation of it, seem to miss this point and always get the head too small and, most times, the legs too long.

144

11

Development of the Modern Head

by Raymond H. Oppenheimer

Lord Gladiator

In 1919 there were many proud and mighty male Bull Terrier lines in both the United States and Britain in which generation succeeded generation in aristocratic triumph: Ch. Norcross Patrician, Ch. Haymarket Faultless, and on to Ch. Norcross Thunderer, Ch. Mascotte Cheeky, Ch. Bloomsbury Cheeky and on to Ch. Coolridge Grit of Blighty, Ch. White Noel and Ch. Krishna. Hampstead Heathen, Robert the Devil, Ch. St. George, Ch. John Ridd and on to Ch. Lord Teddy. There were so many of them and they were so strong and widespread that the onlooker gazing at any one of them might well have exclaimed with Macbeth, "What! will the line stretch out to the crack of doom?"

Certainly it must have seemed that the answer was "Yes," and yet even at that moment those with keen eyes might have seen a cloud "no bigger than a man's hand" from which such a deluge of outstanding champions was to come that in twenty short years every rival male line had been totally submerged.

In 1918 the Great War was reaching its climax when a Bull Terrier was whelped in London with a head far in advance of

145

Lord Gladiator, whelped in 1918, generally credited with being the source of the modern Bull Terrier head.

Another view of Lord Gladiator. The dog shows obvious faults, but his virtues changed the course of the breed.

anything seen before. With men dying in the trenches at the rate of thousands a week, it was impossible for any dog's head, however remarkable, to create much of a stir outside a very limited circle. But by 1919 when peaceful activities were resumed, this dog, bred by the late W. J. Tuck and called Lord Gladiator, started upon his stud career and launched a tail-male line that was to crush its rivals with a speed and ruthlessness that any Juggernaut might have envied.

At first, not unnaturally, nothing very dramatic occurred. Gwent Graphite in the first generation was a good but not outstanding dog. However, his son, Ch. Crooke's Great Boy, was outstanding, though no more so than others had been, but he in his turn did shake up the pundits a little when he sired Ch. White Rose Girl, Egyptian Goddess, and Ch. Galalaw Benefactor, all of which were obviously exceptional. From then on the line gathered pace and power until by 1936 it was clearly dominant.

At this moment, when almost all opposition had already been crushed anyway, except for Ch. Maldwyn, Ch. Midhurst Mercury, and Defender of Monshireval, who were fighting to maintain the Hampstead Heathen line, Lord Gladiator brought up his heaviest guns; in 1937 came Ch. Raydium Brigadier and the Colored Ch. Romany Rhinestone; in 1938, Ch. Velhurst Vindicator; in 1939, Ch. Ormandy's Mr. McGuffin; and that was the end. These four trampled upon their few remaining rivals and Lord Gladiator reigned supreme.

Great or Lucky

Keen students of the breed naturally had all along been asking themselves whether the increasing dominance of Lord Gladiator's line was chance or whether it was the workings of certain definite laws of inheritance applicable to all Bull Terriers and which would therefore prove valid in other cases.

Lord Gladiator was by Ch. Oaksford Gladiator ex Ch. Lady Betty, each by Bloombury Czar and, as we have seen, his claim to fame lay in his exceptional head. In fact, otherwise he was a comparatively ordinary dog. So it followed that, if his value was not chance, the success of his descendants must indicate that a great head, even though accompanied by some unsoundness, was a continuing and valuable asset to a line. At this point observers noted

147

This sketch by Enno Meyer pictures the ideal of the 1930s. The head leans far toward the Terrier type and lacks the strength demanded today.

Ch. White Mischief Maid of Johmad-Ernicor, the best-headed bitch of the early 1940s. By Ch. Pantigon of Enderly ex Barbara Fritchie of Ernicor. Bred by Madalene R. Michaels, and owned by John L. Michaels.

Ch. Cylva Becky Sharpe, born 1930, the best-headed bitch of her generation.

148

three interesting and complementary facts: First, that the breeders who ignored heads in the search for soundness were soon in trouble. Second, that those who used heads and risked some unsoundness were very successful and often got soundness too. And third, that lines that were weak in heads very quickly petered out.

It was only a very short step from that to the inference that good heads were most probably governed by hybrid dominant factors; i.e., they carried with them in recessive form the factors for plainer and plainer heads, and that the breed would always "recede" to the plainer type unless great care was taken to preserve the head which artists had for years portrayed as the ideal but which no one had ever thought fully attainable until Lord Gladiator appeared.

At this point I want to touch very lightly upon the Mendelian law which says that if a dominant factor is present it always manifests itself. That is true if the dominant factor is present in the body cells, but (although I have never seen it stated categorically in a book on genetics) my experience has led me to believe that dominant factors can be absent in the body cells and yet be present in the reproductive cells. That is the only practical explanation I can find of how certain animals pass on factors known to be dominant which they themselves do not possess and it is the only workable theory I can find to explain how some Bull Terriers can transmit great heads although they themselves have very ordinary ones.

I am aware that there is a school of thought which believes that great heads are produced by a process akin to that which produces *agoutism* in rabbits, but I have not found this a workable explanation.

Anyway, for practical purposes I think breeders will do well to accept this theory until a better one is propounded and to draw from it the conclusion which is demonstrable from the records— that there is no hope at all of great headed puppies unless at least one of the grandparents had a great head. That is a point of immense importance and one which should never be overlooked.

Now to return to Lord Gladiator. The facts which I have outlined made it obvious that the triumph of his line was not chance. In any case, successive events both inside and outside his line merely followed a pattern similar to that which observers had already noted. This pattern is plainly and repeatedly observable to this day and makes it clear that breeders who ignore the use of dogs with great heads do so at their peril.

Oliver Ford, current president of the Bull Terrier Club of America, pictured judging at Montgomery County show, awarding ribbon to Ch. Silverwood Fire Belle Clapper. Handler, Bert Tormey. Belle, owned by Mr. and Mrs. Thomas B. Simmons, was Best of Variety at the 1968 Bull Terrier Club Specialty at Ox Ridge—from the classes.

12

How to Judge the Bull Terrier

MANY a judge who does a number of breeds has little relish for a Bull Terrier assignment. The obvious reason is that this is probably the most difficult breed to judge. A man who does not know his business thoroughly can very easily put up the worst dog in the class—or in the show. In fact, I have seen that very thing happen more times than I care to remember. No judge likes to learn after his assignment is finished that he has utterly missed a great one. But even thoroughly experienced judges who are practical breeders may differ widely in placing the same dogs on the same day. This has been shown time after time in England, where a committee of three judges may pick one dog for the Ormandy Jug, and the committee for the Regent Trophy may place the same dog fourth or fifth and put up another dog who had not been in the running for the Jug.

There are four main reasons why it is so difficult to judge Bull Terriers:

The first reason is the wide variation in size allowed by the Standard. Neither the American or the English Standard specifies weight. The judge may be asked to choose between a 30 lb. bitch and a 60 lb. dog. The man who has the two stand side by side, feels the muzzle and forelegs of both, and then comes up with the sixty

151

pounder as the winner because it has the bigger muzzle and heavier bone has done the smaller dog a great injustice—and has done a bad job of judging. The only way to compare the relative strength of muzzle or bone of two specimens of widely differing weight is to stand off and look at them. It is the eye and not the hand which must do the job.

The second reason for the difficulty in judging Bull Terriers is the wide variance in type. On the one side may be a specimen on the Terrier type, and on the other side may be one more "Bull-doggy" in type. One suggests agility, the other suggests power. Which is the better dog?

When the problem is further complicated because the judge has to select between a large dog of the Terrier type and a small dog of the Bulldog type, no wonder he finds his confusion more greatly confounded, unless he knows what to look for.

The third reason is this: Sometimes a judge will completely miss the best one because it is competing against second-rate dogs. Because it is different he feels that it must be further from the Standard than are the poor ones before him, so down will go the better dog. A dog that should never win anything may go over a great one. This is more likely to happen in Bull Terriers than in any other breed, just because the great one may be the only good one in the ring—and the eye of the judge may be thrown off because of the overall impression he gets from the mediocrities.

And the fourth reason is that too often a judge will make his placings on the basis of faults instead of on virtues—on what a dog *is not* rather than on what it *is*. The more the faults and the worse they are, in his opinion, the lower down goes the dog, even though in its virtues it may far excel every other exhibit in the ring. Included in this fourth reason is judging for soundness regardless of type—the easy way out for the judge who does not really know the type points of the breed. I have seen some pretty dreadful things done in the name of soundness.

Type vs. Soundness

Theoretically, the objective of dog shows is to help spot the dogs most likely to make breeding history. Such dogs are those in which are most strongly represented the physical characteristics of the ideal of the breed.

152

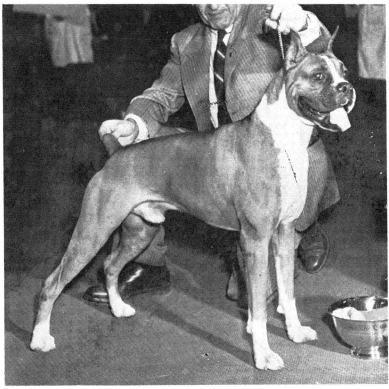

One of the soundest dogs ever whelped—the immortal Boxer, Ch. Bang Away of Sirrah Crest, 121 times Best in Show all-breeds.

Much judging in all breeds is done on the basis of soundness and faults, without much regard for type. That is the easy way to do it. And it is so convenient an excuse to give when questioned—"I couldn't put up a dog with such a bad back line"—or "such a bad rear"—or "with a light eye," etc. Have you ever noticed how rarely a judge will be able to explain why he puts a certain dog *up?* He almost always is far readier to explain why he puts a dog *down.* That certainly is judging in reverse. Why ignore the virtues of the winning dog when explaining why decisions were made as they were? Isn't it far more logical to explain the good points that caused a dog to go *up* rather than why another went *down?*

153

This dog is a very sound Bull Terrier, but lacks any quality in type.

This dog has some great virtues of type, but he also has some pronounced faults.

A lot of breeding is done on that same basis. The judge who bases his decisions on faults is the one most likely to put the worst dog at the top and the best dog at the bottom, just as the breeder who proceeds on that same basis is most likely to wind up at the bottom of the heap.

Suppose we take a dog as sound as they come, a great showman with excellent bone, splendid back line, almost perfection in movement, so well put together that he simply cannot stand wrong. Sounds like a great stud—just what the advocates of soundness in Bull Terriers say they want, doesn't it? The dog we have in mind has practically everything those people want—except type. His picture is on a preceding page—the famous Boxer, Ch. Bang Away of Sirrah Crest, with 121 Bests in Show, all breeds, to his credit.

Tossed in the Bull Terrier ring, Bang Away would logically go to the end of the line even though he might be the soundest dog there. Quite obviously, something more than great physical excellence is necessary to make up a good Bull Terrier.

Next we come to the picture of an unusually sound Bull Terrier, high on leg, deficient in head, obviously very poor in type—but all right in back line, with good coat and splendid gait. This dog in the show ring would be very hard to fault on his structural qualities. Sound as he is, he would be worthless as a stud because he has no virtues of type to throw, and so he is worthless in the show ring. However, in the Bull Terrier ring he would logically place above the sensationally sound Bang Away, for he is of far better Bull Terrier type.

Now we come to a Bull Terrier who at first glance shows a most shockingly bad fault—it would be hard to find a worse back line. It is not too difficult to find other things wrong with him. But we also find a head far above average, a good strong underjaw, good ears—in fact there is a lot of good in this dog once we start to study him. In some respects he is a very good dog indeed, just as in other respects he is a very bad dog indeed.

Which dog should a judge put up: the great physical specimen, Bang Away, the leggy dog with no type but great soundness, or the faulty dog with some true greatness of type about him? There is no more reason to put up the leggy dog than there is to put up Bang Away. Neither has anything to contribute in the way of good Bull Terrier type, and neither if used at stud would produce a Bull Terrier worth looking at a second time.

The dog with the bad back line is something else again. He has a lot to throw, especially in badly needed head qualities. It would seem obvious that he is the only one of the three worth considering for first place in this group of three, because he is the only one who has anything to throw of any real value in the way of type.

It goes without saying that a dog with the structural excellence of the leggy dog plus the virtues of type of the dog with the bad back would be a far better candidate for our blue ribbon or for consideration as a sire. But here we are dealing in extremes in the effort to make a most important point—to drive home the value of type over soundness when it comes to making a decision between them.

In this evaluation of type vs. soundness, from the standpoint of a breeder the virtues and faults in a pedigree play an important part. If we examine the pedigree of the dog with the bad back, we find that his greatest fault is not common to his line. In fact, his line is noted for good backs, good fronts, and good heads; it should be quite easy to breed out the bad back line, which might never occur again in the lifetime of the breeder. When we examine the pedigree of the leggy Bull Terrier, we find nothing in the type of his ancestors that can help us—using him would only put us back in our breeding program.

The following great basic principle, therefore, would seem obvi-

155

ous as a keystone to success either in judging or in breeding: Any decision should always be made in favor of type, because otherwise type will tend to go backwards intsead of forwards. The virtues of type are unusually hard to get and to hold in Bull Terriers. Unless when we find them we recognize them and hold on to them, we will lose them from our line and wind up with stock of no breeding or show value.

But there are certain common denominators of type that help sort out the better dogs, except when it is merely a case of trying to find the least objectionable of a poor lot. In that case, probably the best thing to do is to judge on soundness just because there is no type of any value on which to base a decision.

In the Ring

In every judging assignment there are two basic maxims to keep in mind:

First, to judge the dogs so that the spectator can see what is going on. After all, at a dog show the spectators have paid good money to see the dogs judged.

Second, the judge has a definite responsibility to each exhibitor who has shown him the honor of asking his opinion. He should go over every dog carefully even if it is fourth-rate. The exhibitor quite likely is fond of the dog and considers that it has some very good points; he has paid an entry fee and has spent many hours getting his dog ready for the show, bringing it there, and waiting around at the show itself. The judge owes that exhibitor every consideration while he is in the ring, even though it may be apparent that the exhibitor has brought the dog only to help the breed make a showing. But in addition to being courteous and considerate to each and every exhibitor, the judge must be fair, honest, and courageous. And most judges are just that.

When I judged Scottish Terriers at a match show for the first time, there was a pretty fair entry in dogs and in the Winners' class it finally narrowed down to a choice between two dogs obviously owned by the same person. One was handled by a woman and it was plain that she was the doggy person. Her husband was a fumbler. The tempting thought crossed my mind, "The woman must have what she thinks is the better dog and, as I don't know too much about the breed, it is safer to put her dog up." The more I looked at the two dogs, the more I disagreed with what I thought was the woman's evaluation of her own dogs, and so I put up the dog handled by her husband even though I felt I would be criticized. Sure enough, the woman came over after the judging and said, "Why did you put up the dog handled by my husband?" (which was a very intelligent way to put it). I told her and she said, "I wanted to see what you would say. I gave my husband the better dog hoping that it would win and that it would encourage him to take more interest." Was I relieved!

It sometimes may be a temptation to put up a dog because it has been winning, or because it is owned by a big kennel, or because it is being handled by a professional known only to take in a good one which he is sure will win. Such a temptation is only a very uncertain crutch on which to lean and should be vigorously discarded.

I recall one well-known figure in a certain breed who entered a dog with "particulars unknown." When the judge started to go over the dog, the handler whispered, "You want to go over this one carefully. He is a good one." The dog won its class, to the amusement of the handler, but was never shown again as it was not even purebred!

There is only one way to play safe and that is to put up what you think is the best dog regardless of what is on the other end of the lead. Do a favor for a friend to help him finish and when he leaves he will always wonder if you would not do a greater friend a favor at his expense. If you know why you put a dog up you are on the safest possible ground.

Rarely will everybody agree with you, so that the more you try to please one group, the more you will displease another group. At one show I put a very fine bitch Best of Opposite Sex over a dog I did not like but who on that day was the better of the two. My wife reported to me two conversations she had overheard. One woman said, "How could he ever have put that horrible bitch Best of Opposite Sex?" The other conversation revolved around the comment, "How could he put that lovely bitch down to that terrible dog!" That is what you, as a judge, can sometimes expect in the way of agreement with your judging, and the only person to try to satisfy is yourself.

After all, when one stops to think about it, it is by no means rare for trained experts to disagree. Take prize fights, for example— what a high percentage of split decisions there are, with seldom unanimous agreement as to what rounds each contestant won or lost. Even with our Supreme Court, how often do these legally trained minds fail to agree as to the proper interpretation of the facts laid before them, despite the fact that they have ample opportunity to discuss them! Indeed, it is expecting far too much to demand of the poor judge that he please everybody—including the losers.

In the United States, it is common practice to have the dogs walked in a circle around the ring—even if there is only one dog in the class. If there are several dogs, after walking they should be lined up on one side of the ring, away from the numbered spots. The generally accepted practice in Terriers is for the judge to have each dog brought to him in the center of the ring, instead of having the judge himself walk over to each dog. In addition to conserving the judge's energy, this helps to give the spectators a better view of the dogs, and it gives each dog, in turn, a full opportunity to be in the limelight.

As regards the points to look for: the Bull Terrier always has been essentially a "head breed," whether we like it or not. It is the dogs with the great heads and great type, and not the dogs with great soundness, which have left their mark on the breed. Ch. Ferdinand of Ormandy was perhaps the soundest Bull Terrier I have ever seen, and, yet, where are his descendants? On the other hand, Int. Ch. Raydium Brigadier had a magnificent head, a loose shoulder, a straight stifle, poor rear movement—yet, what a tremendous influence he has exerted on the breed!

When I was in England in 1955 to judge at a championship show—that of the Northern Provincial Bull Terrier Club in Manchester—Raymond Oppenheimer and I had quite a discussion on the theory of judging. He made this analysis of the development of a good judge: In his first phase the judge would put up the dogs that he, as an individual, liked. In his second phase, he would put up the dogs he thought he should put up. And in his third phase, he would put up the dogs which in their make-up had those things most likely to benefit the breed at that particular stage in its evolution. And Mr. Oppenheimer contended that history would show whether or not the judge had put up the right dogs. (This confirms what we have discussed—that it is the greatness of type that must be considered, the things that will benefit the Bull Terrier as a breed.

158

We have only to go back to Westminster winners of the past fifteen years to see which of these winners have made a name for themselves through their progeny and which have dropped into oblivion.)

After which digression, important though it is, let us come back to the details of judging. We must first evaluate the head. But here is one head long and narrow, and over there is one shorter and broader. How do we start?

I must again digress and pass on a bit of advice given me by Mrs. Drury L. Sheraton, who judged many breeds, and who knew Bull Terriers from A to Z. Her advice was to adopt a regular routine and to make that routine a matter of habit by invariably adhering to it. The following is a good routine that will make it easier to really understand a dog after it has been gone over.

First, look at the overall dog, get an idea as to how it is put together, its balance. Is it broad and deep of chest, not too Terrier-like and not too Bulldoggy? How is its back line and shortness of back, its general conformation, the length of what should be a graceful and well proportioned neck, the straightness of its front, the shape and size of the feet (which should be small and cat-like with thick pads), the stifle (which should be well-bent).

After getting that overall picture, go to the head and note the profile—the nearer an arc with a Roman finish, the better; there must be no stop. Note the squareness of jaw as viewed from the side, the strength of the underjaw, the tightness of lip, the fill—the head should be filled right up under and in front of the eyes, e.g., egg-like; the entire muzzle should suggest power without coarseness, for the Bull Terrier is the strongest jawed dog in the Terrier Group.

From the front, note the color, shape, and placement of eye—it should slant down towards the nose and an angle of forty-five degrees is perfect. Note the shape and placement of ears—they should be on top of the head like those of a horse and not on the side of the head like those of a jackass. Examine the bite—it is better to have the handler show you the bite than to open the dog's mouth yourself, as a judge handling mouths is more apt to carry diseases from one dog to another. (The American Kennel Club, in its instructions to judges, has recommended this procedure.)

Every dog in the ring has eyes, ears, a profile, a muzzle. It is easy enough to compare them once you know what to look for. They are common denominators.

Now we have given ourselves a good, detailed start by evaluating the most important part of the dog, the part which is unmistakably Bull Terrier.

Having finished with the head, feel the shoulder blades to note the layback of shoulder. (Now is a good time to go back and study the visualization of the Standard and the chart of the skeleton.) Then feel the strength of bone—bones should be strong and round. Feel the depth of chest and the roundness of barrel. Note the texture and tightness of the coat—it should have a harsh feel, and fit tightly.

Now we go to the back of the dog; we feel the thighs, note the bend of stifle; make sure that the tail does not extend below the hock joint; note its shape (the straighter the tail the better) ; note how it is placed—it should be set on low and appear to be a logical continuation of the spine. A tail that is thin where it joins the body indicates a weak spine.

We now stand in back of the dog and look at its rear. Are the thighs strong and muscular? Are the legs straight? Does this rear appear to be a powerful one, with lines that are clean? If a male, is the dog a monorchid or a cryptorchid? (If there is any doubt, have the ring steward call the veterinarian, for these faults make a dog of any breed ineligible to compete in the United States or England) .

The next thing to do is to take another look at the dog as a whole, so as to fix the component parts in one's mind, and, as the judging progresses, to remember wherein one dog, in the overall picture, may be superior to others—especially in balance and type.

Movement

Then move the dog. He should move straight and true at both ends. When viewed from the side, he should appear to be all in one piece. (In the more important placings, it is a good idea to have the dog moved in an "L" path so that he can be viewed moving from the side as well as going and coming.) The Bull Terrier is more apt to have his feet come under him as he moves (rather than to hang straight down as is the case with other Terriers) as a result of his width of chest and broadness of rear. He was bred and built to do a

160

Pigjaw. The way the underjaw of the Bull Terrier bitch at left slants weakly back suggests the underjaw of the pig at right. The underjaw should be square in profile.

job that is different from that of the Fox Terrier or the Airedale, and this is reflected in his movement, which lacks their preciseness.

The principal test as to true Bull Terrier movement is to keep this always in mind: The job of the Bull Terrier is not to run in the field like a Setter, nor to course like a Greyhound, but to be able to move fast and surely in a small space. His original function was that of a fighting animal and he should be able to move like one. Many

Showing why they are called cow hocks.

161

a dog whose legs move in a perfectly straight line backwards and forwards is actually a weak mover that would lack the speed and power of a dog that might actually weave when asked to trot, a gait he would never use in a fight. This whole subject of Bull Terrier movement is a difficult one to assess, and the eye must be trained to note whether or not the dog moves in a true Bull Terrier fashion—like a powerful fighting dog, but possessed of the graceful surety that breeders have been trying to breed into it.

In the November 18, 1955, issue of the English publication *Our Dogs,* T. J. Horner, one of England's most knowledgeable Bull Terrier people, wrote:

> Can a badly made dog move true? It all depends on what is meant by badly made. In Bull Terriers, type is anything but fixed and varies between the Bulldog and the Greyhound, the ideal being a dog of great power and substance in relatively small compass, yet with the reach of neck and angulation to give it maximum speed and activity.
>
> Therefore, a very Bulldoggy type or a very Greyhoundy type *is badly made for the breed.* Quite often one finds an animal which has the upright shoulder and straight stifle (which go with Bulldog type) and yet moves *true* at both ends. I did not say moves well, because even if it does move true it is bound to lack liberty and length of stride. Again, one often finds a Greyhound type with narrow front, falling croup and long legs, which may be quite sound and true in movement *yet is badly made for the breed.*
>
> To make a good Bull Terrier from either of these types one would have to re-arrange the whole animal, which might take several generations, whereas the slackness or cowhocks in a correctly built one can often be put right in the next generation, many such instances being attributable to bad rearing. Therefore, in my view, a well made one going badly is more desirable than a badly made one going true.

In the same issue and on the same subject, Joanna Chadwick, whose interest lies in Rottweilers, states:

> A judge must, of course, penalize a dog who *stands* cowhocked or with inturned pasterns, as having an actual anatomical disability; but an animal who *naturally stands foursquare* but develops "faulty" movement at certain speeds—perhaps to lose it again at speed—deserves to be looked at a good deal more carefully than many of our learned judges would admit.

Those interested in learning more about movement, so as to be able to discuss the subject with opinions based on facts rather than on guesses, will do well to study *The Dog in Action,* by McDowell Lyon (published by Howell Book House Inc.). This book explains how conformation affects movement, how the angle of the shoulder blade affects the stride, why one dog places his feet in a certain way while another travels differently, the structural difference between the cat foot and the hare foot and why the cat foot is less fatiguing, etcetera.

And now to a very important fact to keep in mind at all times. In the ring, the judge is "the boss." He must keep order in the ring. It is his privilege to order from the ring any handler or dog that is disorderly; if it disturbs the others, he may require a dog to remain out of the ring or to one side until he is ready to judge it. Sometimes a dog may merely be temporarily unruly, but it is not fair to other exhibitors to permit such a dog to upset the entire ring, and a momentary withdrawal may be all that is necessary to restore order.

Ch. Carlcres Carefree going BOV at Golden State Bull Terrier Specialty in California. Author Ernest Eberhard is the judge, and handling Carefree is the importer Mrs. Yearsley.

Ch. Coolyn North Wind, winner of the BCoA Specialty
1939 and 1940, Isis Vabo Trophy 1939, 1940 and 1941.
North Wind weighed 38 pounds.

Eng. Ch. Raydium Enterprise of Ormandy, weight 70 lbs. Believed to be the
largest English champion.

13

This Matter of Weight

EVERY standard developed for the Bull Terrier has avoided any limitation of weight which would have any practical significance. The 1915 American Standard at first allowed a variation of between twelve pounds and sixty pounds, then raised the lower limit to twenty-five pounds with not even a mention in "Faults" of a penalty for weights above sixty pounds or below twenty-five pounds. Thus the weights stipulated became "preferred" weights and not limitations. The current English Standard blithely ignores any weight preference, as does the English version proposed in 1956. And so the judge of Bull Terriers must function without the slightest clue as to what the height or weight of the ideal Bull Terrier should be—except for his own personal preferences.

What should the weight limitations be? Any attempt to set a limitation is quite likely to run up against the prejudice of the individual fancier, who may say to himself, "That's not the weight of my dog and so it is wrong."

At a meeting of the Bull Terrier Club of America a motion was once made that the Standard include the following:

"Preferred weight. For males, between 50 and 55 lbs.; for bitches, 40 to 45 lbs. In judging, weight to be disregarded in favor of type and soundness."

The motion fell flat.

Nancy Hanks of Ernicor, two years old, 30 pounds. Born in 1934.

The basic reasons for the motion, as given in the Club's minutes, contain some interesting facts:

"The proposed new English Standard makes no mention of weight despite the fact that the Bull Terrier has a far wider variation in weight than has any other breed. Many breeders have long been of the opinion that a closer limitation of weight would be of distinct help as an aid towards insuring a greater uniformity of type. Most of the better males run between 50 and 55 lbs., though the English Ch. Enterprise of Ormandy weighed 70 lbs. and Ch. Coolyn North Wind, 50 times breed winner, weighed 38 lbs. The better bitches generally run between 40 and 45 lbs., though Int. Ch. Fautless of Blighty weighed around 60 lbs. and Ch. Coolyn Crepe Suzette weighed about 25 lbs. Since type and soundness are of far greater importance than weight, it seemed wise in suggesting these 'Preferred Weights' to add the qualification that 'In judging, these preferred weights shall be disregarded in favor of type and soundness.' "

I have seen Bull Terriers as heavy as 85 lbs. In fact, in New York City some forty years ago I saw one as large as a Great Dane. When any breed starts to get too large or too small, it begins to lose its essential character even though individual specimens may be entirely acceptable.

The Bull Terrier was originally bred to do a certain job. A dog much under 35 lbs. does not have enough power to do the job, just as a dog much over 60 lbs. is apt to be too slow for the job. A weight of 50 to 55 lbs. for males seems to be close to the ideal, as does 40 to

45 lbs. for bitches. Such dogs or bitches are small enough to have sufficient agility for the purpose, and large enough to have sufficient weight to give authority to their speed and power. These weights seem to be the natural limits between which the breed is most likely to function at its best and therefore to appear to the eye to be at its best. And right there we run smack up against the universal tradition that a good Bull Terrier is a good Bull Terrier no matter what its weight.

It seems essentially wrong to me to breed without any ideal in the matter of weight, and to have litters wherein weights may vary from 30 pounds to 55 lbs. It complicates breeding, as frequently the dog is too big for the bitch to permit of an easy service. It complicates judging, as a wide weight variation increases the complexities of the job. And it complicates the proper development of type, as there is more likely to be a wider variation between the niceties of type in extreme sizes than between those of a closer weight.

Mr. Douglas Lindsay, M.D., F.R.F.P.S., F.R.C.O.G., in the *Annual* of the Bull Terrier Club of England for 1948–49, states: "Controversy on the height and weight proper to a Bull Terrier has, like an endemic disease, always been active, reaching at times epidemic proportions, notably in 1895, 1906 and 1925. The epidemic of 1948 may, however, surpass all these earlier outbreaks. . . . There are no reliable data of earlier champions by which the student breeder can reconstruct them in proportion and balance for comparison with the modern dog. This is a sorry example of missed opportunity and explains how a commendable canvass of breeders and owners made by a breed club in 1946 on the height-weight problem produced suggested weights so varied that it was impossible to take any effective step towards standardization."

Mr. Lindsay was appointed by the Bull Terrier Club to work out a measuring system and forms for the recording of proper statistics, especially of the winners of the Ormandy Jugs and the Regent Trophy. In his words, "Annually this journal will tabulate the statistics for the previous year." Unfortunately for the welfare of the breed, this very commendable project seems to have fallen by the wayside.

So, as somebody must take the bull by the horns some day if anything constructive is ever to be accomplished, I hereby recommend the consideration of 50 to 55 lbs. for males and 40 to 45 lbs. for bitches—and forthwith retire to a bombproof shelter.

A very practical whelping box, 3 feet by 3 feet. Three sides are no more than 6 inches wide. The fourth side has a 6-inch board and a 4-inch board. After a few days, remove the 4-inch board to make the area for the dogs larger. When the puppies open their eyes, remove one of the 6-inch sides, so that the puppies can explore the "wide world" and then return to sleep. The entire box is hinged, so that when not needed, it can be folded to put away.

14

Breeding Bull Terriers

WHY is it that so often top stock will be imported into the United States—and peter out within two or three generations? Why is it that even in England, where the very best studs are available to everybody within a reasonable distance and at a low cost, some breeders in over twenty years of active breeding have never bred a champion? Why is it that some breeders will have at least one worthy champion in almost every litter? Is it luck—or is it something else?

Basic Reasons for Success or Failure

The whole foundation of breeding is so fluid that it is possible to cite numerous important exceptions to every rule that can be advanced, and so cast doubt upon its validity. However, when we analyze the reasons for the success or the lack of success of the individual breeder, we find that there is one reason which will stand up in a sufficient number of cases to warrant the most careful consideration—and which will come as close to proving itself as is possible with any breeding idea. That reason falls into two parts:

1. The average (and unsuccessful) breeder will breed *against* what he does *not* like and not *for* what he *does* like. That is, he will

breed *against* the bad rear and poor backline that he does *not* want instead of for the great head and expression that he *does* want.

2. Too many breeders do not know a good dog when they see one: they can recognize common faults apparent in any breed, but they have not trained themselves to recognize the virtues of type that we have previously discussed. It is absolutely vital to be able to recognize such virtues if one is to be a successful breeder or a capable judge.

Listen to comments around any judging ring. The "expert" comment is usually a savage criticism of the top dogs—straight stifles, bad movement, crooked fronts, etc. Seldom indeed is there any recognition of a strong, square underjaw; of a beautifully shaped cat-foot; of a properly shaped and placed ear; of the balance and spirited movement that is the birthright of a good Bull Terrier. The average breeder unconsciously trains himself to see the bad in a dog rather than the good, and so faults assume a far greater importance in his eyes than they should.

Take, for example, Int. Ch. Kashdowd's White Rock of Coolyn Hill, a truly great dog who in England won both the Regent Trophy and the Ormandy Jug; who in the United States went Best in Show, all breeds, when he was first shown July 17, 1954; and who, after being shown sixty-eight times, had chalked up ten best in show awards, all breeds, twenty-four Terrier Groups firsts—a remarkable record for any breed. Such comments were heard about him as "too short in head," "body too long," "moves badly in rear," "front is crooked," "bad ears," etc. But after the dog had time after time defeated every other Bull Terrier sent against him, placed nearly every time in the Terrier Group, and was piling up a Best in Show record that had never even been approached in Bull Terriers, it began to become too obvious that the "experts" did not know what they were talking about.

That pattern of inability to recognize virtues is so common that further examples are not necessary—they are apparent on every hand and in every breed. Now, when this inability to recognize virtues is carried over into breeding, we begin to see why the breeder who cannot recognize the virtues to breed to, but who breeds against the common faults he recognizes, is doomed to failure. He may need to improve heads—but will refuse to breed to a great headed dog who may have a poor rear. Or if he does by chance breed a great headed bitch, he will discard it because of its faults. And so we find him gradually losing the virtues which are so precious and so rare, and breeding ever poorer stock with each generation.

If the ideas of the relatively unsuccessful breeders had been followed by the successful breeders, the greatest Bull Terriers ever bred would never have been whelped.

Take, for example, the English Ch. The Sphinx—the first Bull Terrier to twice top the breed at Crufts. His dam had a blue eye, as did the dam of one of England's greatest studs and an Ormandy Jug Winner, Ch. Ormandy Sylveston Starshine. Or take the English Ch. Ormandy Souperlative Snow Flash, a Regent Trophy winner—his dam was undershot; this dog is proving to be a great stud force and sired the sensational litter sisters Ch. Phidgity Snow Dream and Ch. Phidgity Flashlight of Wentwood.

Or consider Ch. Romany Reliance, the source of great heads—neither his rear nor his mouth was his fortune and his tail-set was akin to that of a cow. Or Rubislaw, whose disposition was so bad that he could not complete his championship, yet was the major source of substance. Or take one of the key matings in Bull Terriers, one of such great importance that Mrs. Drury L. Sheraton, one of our truly great authorities, told me many years ago never to consider any Bull Terrier without this mating in its pedigree—Ambassador and Ivy Gladiator. But Ambassador had two blue eyes! Ambassador was the sire of the great Ch. Cylva Belle and she was the aunt of Ch. Rhoma, whom some consider the best bitch ever bred. Indeed, if this dog with two walleyes had never been mated to Ivy Gladiator, it would have been a sad loss to the breed.

There is an endless list of great sires and dams, who, in themselves or in their immediate background, had what the unsuccessful breeder would regard as an unsurmountable fault to his using it as a breeding prospect. Yet, the obvious faults in those dogs and bitches mentioned were far overbalanced by their possession of something that was badly needed in the breed—they had a lot to give. Those who breed *against* faults would turn them down. Those who breed *for* virtue would use them eagerly. And history tells which are right.

When a certain virtue is so hard to get as it is in Bull Terriers, then that virtue must be grasped whenever it occurs, even though it

171

may mean the temporary toleration of great faults. If the virtue is not grasped, then obviously it will disappear.

It is absolutely vital in breeding to be able to recognize those precious virtues, to realize their importance if progress is to be made, to try to hold those virtues and seek to eliminate in future matings any faults which may have crept in due to their presence in the stock used. There is no such thing as a perfect dog and so any dog used will have faults which may be more or less serious. If there are not great virtues present, then quite obviously the virtues are unlikely to be present in the offspring and will not linger in any strain which is bred *against* faults instead of *for* virtues.

I am inclined to think that sometimes a bad fault may not be due to heredity but to feeding or environment. For example, loose feet or a crooked front may be due to rickets resulting from lack of proper food or sunshine. Cowhocks may come from much standing on the hind legs during puppyhood. "Out-at-shoulder" may come because a puppy is constantly leaning down to look under something to get a better look at the outside world.

We all know that the parts of puppies grow at different rates of speed. That is, ears grow faster than the rest of the body; the underjaw grows more slowly than the upper jaw, as indicated by the fact that badly overshot puppies often wind up with a perfect bite. (Yet an undershot puppy at three months may have a level bite at eight months.) Now, if sickness strikes a puppy so that growth is affected at the time a certain part would normally be developing, then that part may never have the opportunity to grow into its normal proporation.

These observations are not presented as facts, since the number of cases on which they are based are too few to permit of more than an educated guess, but they may suggest a line of observation to others that will result in greater knowledge for us all.

Support for the preceding paragraphs is to be found in an article in the *Ladies Home Journal* for June 1956, called "The Uninsulted Child." It discusses a theory first stated by Dr. Theodore H. Ingalls, Associate Professor at the Harvard School of Public Health, and the article is well worth reading. In a nutshell, this theory states that shock to or illness of the mother during human pregnancy can seriously affect the unborn child so that it may come into the world cursed with a physical deformity even of so serious a nature as Mongoloidism. Dr. Ingalls also voices the theory that any effect on

172

the supply of oxygen during pregnancy can result in mental defects, miscarriage, or death within a few weeks after birth. He advises against an airplane trip of any duration during pregnancy. (This indicates that a bitch in whelp should not be flown to its new home.)

The "Genetic Shadow"

The mating of two dogs with perfect fronts will sometimes produce a litter with mostly bad fronts. Why? And why will the mating of good headed stock often produce progeny with poor heads or the mating of poor headed dogs sometimes produce a dog with a great head? There is a scientific basis for all the unexpected results which make the best laid plans "gang oft aglee."

Every dog is actually two dogs. One is the dog which is visible to the eye. The other is the invisible but powerful "genetic shadow" of that dog—the make-up of the genes which determine the characteristics of the progeny which he or she will throw. In this make-up of the genes, the family is of greater importance than is the individual dog in the great majority of cases. It is rare that a sire will stamp himself visibly on his offspring. Probably one of the best examples of throwing his likeness was the Boxer, Ch. Bank Away of Sirrah Crest.

Let us consider some of the many practical examples of genetic problems which we have all experienced.

Marks on the head are recessive. For several generations all parents and offspring may be pure white. Suddenly, head marks may appear. In fact, it is entirely possible that every one of the litter may be marked even though behind the litter there are several generations of pure white stock.

Sometimes a body mark will appear from stock that for generations has had no body marks. Where such markings come from, and exactly why, nobody really knows, although as they are a recessive trait the conditions may have momentarily become favorable for their reappearance.

A non-genetic reason, and one that experienced breeders are familiar with, is that there is a constant tendency to pull towards the past—it is the "drag" of the breed, and it is particularly strong in Bull Terriers where there is such a wide variation in size and type.

173

It is this "drag" of the breed that goes far to explain why so often an American breeder will import top stock only to find that within two or three generations he will be back where he started from, even though he may also import bitches suitable to the stud. The basic reason for the loss of quality, leaving breeding skill out of the discussion, has already been explained—offspring may be selected which have qualities preferred by the breeder but which actually are qualities of a day gone by. Therefore, selection is made of the worst breeding stock in the litter—at least so far as type is concerned—and thus the breeding program will go down hill rapidly.

This down-hill speed may be further accelerated by the breeder who gets a great head or other rare and desirable quality accompanied by a blue eye, a cowhock, or other fault, and he will refuse to breed such a specimen because he has no use for any dog with a bad fault. As a consequence, the virtue of the great head will be quickly lost from the line, and litters of nonentities will be the result.

There are four points on which every successful breeding program is based:

1. Selection.
2. Perseverance.
3. Knowledge of type. (The ability to recognize a good one.)
4. An understanding of how a line is built.

Let us take an example. An intelligent breeding is made, and the resulting litter is not what was expected—there is nothing on the surface worth retaining. So the entire litter is sold and the breeder tries another mating, quite likely with the same result.

That litter which, from its physical appearance, holds no promise is quite likely to be full of promise because of the unseen genetic forces that have been brought into it. The "genetic shadow" probably has been strengthened and improved. Perseverance in the breeding program is almost certain, sooner or later, to result in success. This is true because as each successive breeding is made, the "genetic shadow" of what is wanted becomes stronger and stronger until the desired characteristics almost have to pop out. (Provided, of course, that the breedings have been made intelligently and with a full knowledge of the family lines involved.)

An examination of the pedigrees of the great dogs of the past will

Ch. Coolyn Bailfire, famous sire of the 1930s. Bred by Mrs. Jessie Bennett.

testify to the truth of that basic principle we have been discussing. A pedigree may be full of gods of no great show importance—but suddenly the "genetic shadow" becomes so strong and so improved that the line will start to produce truly great ones.

This brings us back again from a different angle to that most important fact we discussed in a previous chapter—to breed for virtues and not for an absence of faults. It cannot be too strongly emphasized that if a virtue is not bred for, it will be lost. If only breeders would realize the importance of that principle and hold fast to it, everybody who tries to breed better dogs would benefit and much faster progress would be possible.

And now here is another fact whose importance is not generally realized: the fault in the dog with great virtue may not appear in the subsequent litter and, in fact, may occur less often in future litters than it will if a dog without that fault is used.

A good example of the workings of that principle was Ch. Coolyn Bailfire, a great American sire of the thirties who gave champions to breeders who never before had bred one—and that in a day when Bull Terrier champions were far harder to make than they are today. Yet, many breeders refused to use him because he had soft ears, and at that time poor ears were a very bad fault. Despite his physical lack, in his "genetic shadow" this dog was strong for good ears and generation after generation traced their good ears back to him. I doubt if he ever threw more than three offspring who did not have unusually good ears, and I further doubt if there was any sire

175

Eng. & Am. Ch. Raydium Brigadier, Regent Trophy 1937.

of his generation who threw such a high percentage of good ears. Those who did not use Bailfire missed a great breeding opportunity.

What makes the whole subject of genetics so difficult to grasp in a practical sense is that there are very few if any characteristics governed by a single gene. We learn *how* things happen and *why* they happen, but know far too little about *how to make them happen.*

We have no accurate list of dominant or recessive characteristics, and things may not always be as they appear. A fault may be caused by environment or by feeding, as previously mentioned, or by both, and so may be disregarded in any breeding program. However, even if the theory of bad feeding and environment as the cause of some physical faults if finally proved true beyond question—and I have seen much evidence to support it—yet the fact remains that the line may have a tendency towards the fault and require only a favorable atmosphere to develop it.

We do know that bad mouths, ticks, and walleyes are recessive. Other characteristics may be both dominant and recessive. Since a characteristic may be governed by a number of genes, the combinations of what may come out are almost endless, both for good and for evil. If one tries to be more theoretical than practical, he can easily get lost in a bewildering maze. It is all far more complicated than when dealing with the simplicities of Mendel's peas. The best thing to do is to breed for the virtues and avoid the faults, but to

176

put up with a fault when this is the only way a virtue can be held or acquired.

An interesting summary of dominant and recessive traits has been worked out by the Eugenics Record Office staff as follows:

Dominant Traits

1. The trait does not skip a generation.
2. On the average, a relatively large number of the progeny are affected.
3. Only affected individuals carry the trait.
4. With traits of this sort, there is less danger of continuing undesirable characteristics in a strain than is the case with recessive traits.
5. The breeding formula for each individual is quite certain.

Recessive Traits

1. The trait may skip one or more generations.
2. On the average, a relatively small percentage of the individuals in the strain carry the trait.
3. Only those which carry a *pair* of determiners of the trait will exhibit it.
4. Those carrying only one determiner can be ascertained only by mating, hence there is much more danger of insidiously contaminating the strain than is the case with dominant traits.
5. The trait must come from both sides of the family.

In the scheme of breeding to establish a line, inbreeding, outcrossing, and line breeding each have their proper place. Let us consider a practical example showing how a line was actually developed to produce top dogs—including what up to that time had been the only two American-bred Bull Terriers to go Best in Show, all breeds.

We will start with the best in show dog, Ch. Heir Apparent to Monty-Ayr, widely known as "Bat." His sire was Int. Ch. Raydium Brigadier, a double grandson of the Regent Trophy winner Ch. Gardenia Guardsman, who was a double grandson of Regent Pluto. Bat's dam, Tanark Queen Mother, was a granddaughter of Ch.

177

Ch. Babylon Ace of Monty-Ayr,
a breed winner at Westminster.

Gardenia Guardsman. Right here we have line breeding to a great English sire. Bat was outcrossed to Buxton Jane Arden, a daughter of Canadian Ch. Brickstop Spitfire, and a brother and sister of this outcross (Ch. The Sorceror of Monty-Ayr and White Princess of Monty-Ayr) were bred together to produce another Best in Show dog, Ch. Forecast of Monty-Ayr. Forecast, mated to his litter sister (Ch. Blonde Bombshell of Monty-Ayr), produced a litter of eight, of which seven finished their championships; the eighth died of a virus disaease before it was a year old; all of the seven won or placed in one or more Terrier Groups.

Bat was again outcrossed to Buxton Katisha, a granddaughter and a double great-granddaughter of Int. Ch. Shure Thing. A bitch from this litter (White Lassie of Monty-Ayr) was mated to Forecast, which was close line breeding. A dog from this litter was Ch. Babylon Ace of Monty-Ayr, best Bull Terrier at Westminster.

Once again Bat was outcrossed—this time to Molly Pitcher of Ernicor. One result of this litter was Ch. Elsie Dinsmore of Ernicor. Elsie was mated to Ch. Babylon Ace of Monty-Ayr, which was close line breeding, and the result was Ch. Madame Pompadour of Ernicor, a bitch who finished her championship with four consecutive five point shows and who broke all Bull Terrier show records for her sex with 80 Best of Variety wins and more Group placings than scored by any other Bull Terrier bitch.

Pompadour was outcrossed to Int. Ch. Braxentra Balechin and one result was Int. Ch. Stormalong's Jewel of Ernicor. As the result

178

of another outcross to Int. Ch. Kashdowd's White Rock, she produced Ch. Davy Crockett of Ernicor, who, at nine months of age, went best Bull Terrier at Westminster.

Here in these examples we find line breeding so close that it is practically inbreeding, and outcrossing—all employed to introduce needed qualities and to develop and fix certain qualities, yet without any loss of fertility, intelligence, or health.

What makes this particularly interesting is the fact that although Int. Ch. Raydium Brigadier was used at stud countless times, this is the only line in which his descendants were intensively inbred, and it is by far the most successful line from him in this country. Inbreeding brought out and intensified the qualities he had to pass on, whereas line breeding and outcrossing largely dissipated them.

Let me emphasize—select for what you want on the basis of knowing what is usually thrown by the stock used. A dog who generally throws good heads is quite likely to throw good heads with your bitch. If he often throws bad ears, he will probably throw bad ears with your bitch, unless her "genetic shadow" for ears is strong enough to overcome his deficiency.

Take plenty of time to study what is needed and what dogs are most likely to give it. Work to a planned program, not to a series of haphazard matings, and the gods are likely to send their sweetest smiles in your direction.

Ch. Madame Pompadour of Ernicor, seen (at left) at 11 weeks, and (right) at six months of age.

179

Eng. Ch. Ormandy's Mr. McGuffin, Regent Trophy 1939 and a great sire.

15

Twenty Basic Breeding Principles

by Raymond H. Oppenheimer

THERE are a vast number of different breeding methods, some good, some bad. I should never presume to try to tell fanciers what is the right method because there is no such thing. Outstanding success can be achieved and has been achieved in a variety of different ways, so all I am going to do is to make some suggestions which I think helpful and to warn against certain pitfalls which trap too many of the unwary.

1. Don't make use of indiscriminate outcrosses. A judicious outcross can be of great value, an injudicious one can produce an aggregation of every imaginable fault in the breed.

2. Don't line breed just for the sake of line breeding. Line breeding with complementary types can bring great rewards; with unsuitable ones it will lead to immediate disaster.

3. Don't take advice from people who have always been unsuccessful breeders. If their opinions were worth having they would have proved it by their successes.

4. Don't believe the popular cliché about the brother or sister of the great champion being just as good to breed from. For every one that is, hundreds are not. It depends on the animal concerned.

5. Don't credit your own dogs with virtues they don't possess. Self-deceit is a stepping stone to failure.

6. Don't breed from mediocrities; the absence of a fault does not in any way signify the presence of its corresponding virtue.

7. Don't try to line breed to two dogs at the same time; you will end by line breeding to neither.

8. Don't assess the worth of a stud dog by his inferior progeny. All stud dogs sire rubbish at times; what matters is how good their best efforts are.

9. Don't allow personal feelings to influence your choice of a stud dog. The right dog for your bitch is the right dog, whoever owns it.

10. Don't allow admiration of a stud dog to blind you to his faults. If you do you will soon be the victim of auto-intoxication.

11. Don't mate together animals which share the same fault. You are asking for trouble if you do.

12. Don't forget that it is the whole dog that counts. If you forget one virtue while searching for another you will pay for it.

13. Don't search for the perfect dog as a mate for your bitch. The perfect dog (or bitch) doesn't exist, never has and never will!

14. Don't be frightened of breeding from animals that have obvious faults so long as they have compensating virtues. A lack of virtues is far the greatest fault of all.

15. Don't mate together non-complementary types. An ability to recognize type at a glance is a breeder's greatest gift; ask the successful breeders to explain this subject—there is no other way of learning. (I would define non-complementary types as ones which have the same faults and lack the same virtues.)

16. Don't forget the necessity to preserve head quality. It will vanish like a dream if you do.

17. Don't forget that substance plus quality should be one of your aims. Any fool can breed one without the other!

18. Don't forget that a great head plus soundness should be another of your aims. Many people can never breed either!

19. Don't ever try to decry a great Bull Terrier. A thing of beauty is not only a joy forever but a great Bull Terrier should be a source of aesthetic pride and pleasure to all true lovers of the breed.

20. Don't be satisfied with anything but the best. The second best is never good enough.

Ch. The Ink Spot of Nelloyd as
a four-months-old puppy.

183

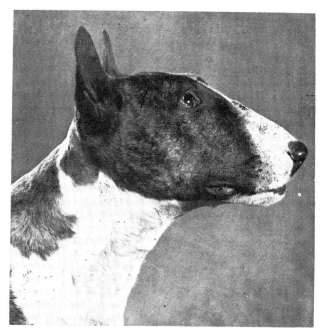

Eng. and Am. Ch. Romany Remarkable, star of the 1950 era.
Imported by Mr. and Mrs. Percy Davis.

No breeder of the Colored Variety has shown such consistent success as has Miss D. Montague Johnstone, whose "Romany" prefix is known the world over. Dogs carrying this prefix are not only milestones in the progress of the Colored Variety, but are now also milestones in the progress of the White Variety, since the interbreeding of Whites, Coloreds, and Color-bred Whites has come into favor on both sides of the Atlantic. Her experience in breeding to produce a desired result, as well as her remarks on the breeding history of the Coloreds, are of considerable practical as well as historical value.

16

Breeding for Color

by Miss D. Montague Johnstone

IT is not difficult to understand how color works—what two colors mated together can or cannot produce—yet it is remarkable how ignorant many breeders still are on this interesting question.

The two most important facts are these:

1. Brindle Is the Dominant Color

That is to say that if a dog* carries the factor for brindle, it will dominate any of the other colors the dog may also carry, and the dog will be brindle in color.

In reverse, if the dog is not brindle (or black-brindle) in color, then, quite obviously, he does not carry the brindle factor. Therefore, if two non-brindles (say two reds, or two fawns, or a red to a tricolor) are mated together, they will produce no brindle or black-brindle puppies, since neither of them carries the factor for brindle.

* The word "dog" covers both sexes as regards color, since in both sexes color behaves exactly alike.

185

It is not necessary for both parents to carry the brindle factor; it is sufficient for one parent to carry it.

Because it is only possible to produce brindle if one or both parents carry the color, brindle is, of all colors, the most easily lost.

Since brindle is, of all colors, the most desired and most popular, it is essential that all serious breeders of Colored Bull Terriers should make it their first aim to retain and preserve this color above all others. This is important.

It is interesting to note that I have seen an odd-colored, almost pale liver-colored bitch with liver nose, who, mated to a Pure White red dog, produced a high percentage of brindle pups. The answer to this one is that either a brindle dog (kept on the place but sworn to have had no part in it) did have a part in the breeding, unknown to the breeder, or that these very rare dilute livers do carry the brindle factor. I am inclined to this latter view, but it must be understood that this is the rarest of rare exceptions that merely prove the rule. I have only seen three or four of these "livers" in nearly thirty years.

2. White, Mated to White, Will Always Produce 100% White Litters

This fact is the stumbling block of many breeders, for they do not appear to be able to comprehend it. It does not matter if the two Whites mated are both Color-Bred, with or without head marks. It does not mater if they have four rich colored brindle and white parents, they will still only produce whites, with or without head marks, according to their strain and its tendency to produce head marks or not. The information given above has been known and well proved for very many years.

The next important point is quite a new find: it is the extreme value of the cbw carrying brindle as a mate for the tricolor or black and tan. Later in this chapter I mention that Romany Rough Weather and Romany Rather Lovely had a tricolor sister. She was a very good bitch and if we had known then what we know now, might have become as famous as the other two. Mated to brindles, her color results were always bad. What she should have been mated to was a cbw carrying brindle, when she would undoubtedly have given us a high percentage of beautifully marked brindle pups.

The first notable example of that combination is English and American Ch. Romany Remarkable. Her dam was a black and tan (solid) and she was mated to Ch. Romany Reprieved (cbw), known to carry brindle very strongly. The result was an equal percentage of rich brindles and bright reds, well marked.

I have seen several other excellent examples, of which the most interesting are as follows:

Ch. Rickmay Rising Star, all white cbw (by the pws Ch. Ormandy Silveston Starshine, ex the cbw Ch. Rickmay Anbanaad), mated to a tricolor bitch, produced a high percentage of rich brindle and white pups. The brindle here managed to come strongly through the sire, with nothing to show for it in the first two generations except a little brindle on Anbanaad's ear! Another interesting example was a tricolored bitch, who, mated first to a rich brindle and white son of the brindle Romany Roast Goose, produced ten pups, and gave the usual bad result: nothing but whites and blacks. Mated a second time to Ch. Romany Repeat Performance (cbw carrying brindle strongly) the same bitch produced eleven pups, five of which were beautifully marked brindles, the remainder being white.

The cbw-carrying-brindle is therefore without doubt exactly what is required as a mate for tricolor or black and tan and, as such, gives the very best possible color result.

While on the question of Colored Whites, it is worth mentioning again that all such are genetically Colored Bull Terriers and when bred to Colored mates, act as if they actually showed their color. Many of them do show color, of course, as they have head marks. According to the color of the head mark, so will they act when mated to Colored mates, Thus, if a cbw carries a brindle head mark, he will act as a brindle; if red, as a red (in which case, of course, he will not produce brindles to a Colored bitch unless she is brindle, because he will act like a red who cannot produce brindle alone).

The all white cbw also carries color (see perfect example of Ch. Rickmay Rising Star, given previously) but the difficulty with them is that one cannot be sure what color they are until tested, which means mating them to a Colored but non-brindle mate. If he gets brindles to such a mate, then he carries brindle.

Needless to say, the cbw who carries brindle is of greater breeding value to breeders of Coloreds than is the cbw who does not. For the breeder of Whites, it does not matter, since whatever color they may carry, they will still produce only white litters from white mates.

Next we come to the "solid" colors, as against the color with white markings.

For the show ring we much prefer and breed for the beautifully marked dog—nice white blaze, white chest and feet, as being very showy and attractive in appearance, and drawing attention to profile and head. Dogs so marked, however, will always throw a percentage of white pups if mated to anything except a solid color. Since breeders of Colored Bull Terriers want colored pups, the solid colored dog is of very great breeding value, although he is at a disadvantage in the show ring with no white to show him off.

A dog that is "solid for color" can almost always be recognized on sight. There is very rarely any need to test him out. He can be any color, brindle, black-brindle, red, fawn, or black and tan. He will have very little, usually no white, on face, and very little or none on chest or legs. Such a dog or bitch will never sire or whelp a white puppy, no matter what he or she is mated to, and this includes matings with Pure White Bull Terriers.

Some dogs can carry quite a lot of white on their chest and still be solid for color. Romany Rivet and Contango Cobblestone are two such examples, but neither had a white blaze. Ch. Romany Rhinestone had not only a white chest, but also white on his face and legs; yet, he never sired a white puppy. In my opinion, this was because he was really very nearly one of the rare "livers." But not quite, since he never sired a brindle puppy to a non-brindle mate. His son, Ch. Romany Roman, was another solid for color, but he was expected to be since he had no blaze and very little white elsewhere.

These "solid" dogs and bitches are the ones to breed from above all others when a breeder feels his strain is getting too many white or badly marked pups, and for this purpose they are of immense value.

To conclude, here is a list of the colors that appear in the Bull Terrier breed:

Brindle, and Brindle and White. All shades, from very dark, through reddish, to golden and silver.

Black-Brindle, and Black-Brindle and White. Here the dog is black, with or without white markings, and carries on his cheeks, inside of front legs and on thighs, definite brindle color, varying in shade as above.

Red Smut, or Red Smut and White. The body is red, with or without white markings, and the mask and eyebrows shaded in black, the tail also usually being dark.

Fawn Smut, or Fawn Smut and White. Similar to the reds, except that the body color is fawn.

Clear Red and White. Similar to the *red smut and white,* but without the black mask and shadings.

Clear Fawn and White. Similar to the *fawn smut and white,* but without the black mask and shadings. (For breeding purposes the *smuts* are usually more valuable than the *clears,* being stronger for color.)

Tricolor. Black, with tan or red points on cheeks, eyebrows, inside of front legs and on thighs. White on face, chest, and feet.

Black and Tan. As above, but with no white blaze, and very little white elsewhere, a "solid" color.

I have put these *tricolors* and *black and tans* last, but in actual fact, now that we know what they can do when mated to cbw carrying brindle, they are of greater breeding value than the *clear reds* and *fawns,* and probably as valuable as the *smuts.* They are not, however, so popular in the show ring, and (although a good dog can never be a bad color and should always be put over a less good dog of another color) they are not to me, and to many others, so typical in appearance, and a good one has to be a little better than his rival to look as good.

189

Examples of Results When Various Colors Are Mated Together:

It must be remembered always that although we can say what two colors mated together can and cannot produce, it depends enormously on the individuals mated as to what, within the rules which have been set out above, they do produce. That is to say, they will not produce what they are unable to produce, but they can quite often disappoint by not producing what they are able to produce, which is probably what you particularly wanted from them. This is because some dogs and bitches are weak, where others are strong in their ability to produce the brindle factor, whether directly through themselves or through their mates.

It is possible, for instance, to have two brindle and white bitches carrying behind them the same proportion of brindle blood. When these are mated to the same dog, whatever his color, one bitch may always give an excellent percentage of brindles while the other may fail to do so.

It is also a fact that the same pair can be mated on two occasions and give entirely different color results in the two resulting litters. The percentage of brindles in one litter may be excellent, and in the other very poor. This serves to show very clearly that one can never exactly forecast a result.

Brindle and White to Brindle and White: A fairly equal proportion of all colors, including white, can be expected. (This mating is not one of our favorites, unless at least two of the grandparents are white, as a concentration of brindle is inclined to lose type. It is also inclined to produce rather a high percentage of black-brindles, who are not as popular as the true brindles, although, personally, I greatly like a well marked one.)

Solid Brindle to Brindle and White: As above, but with a higher percentage of true brindles and no whites. The same remark regarding type is applicable here.

Brindle and White to Red and White, or to Fawn and White, or to Red Smut, or to Fawn Smut: Usually the best combinations, giving good shades of all colors, including whites. Particularly good if a smut is used to a brindle and white, or solid brindle to a red and white or fawn and white, smut or clear.

190

Tricolor, or Black and Tan: Mate to Color Bred White carrying brindle, and expect a good percentage of brindles, with bright reds, and (with the tricolor, not with the black and tan) whites. Colors always tend to be bright when they get, as in this combination, a strong dose of black and white blood.

I have never seen a warm color produced from two cold colors, and I doubt if it is possible, though I do not consider that I have enough evidence to say it definitely is not possible.

We have mated silver brindle to fawns on many occasions, the result has always been silvers, fawns, and whites, never warm shades of brindle, or reds. A brilliant shade of red can always be achieved by mating red to white for several generations, though it is not recommended, as obviously the brindle factor is lost.

> Author's Note. With an understanding of the "how" and the "why" of breeding Coloreds, let us delve into the history of the Variety and examine practical examples which illustrate the results of what Miss Montague Johnstone has learned from the experience of many years. Much of the following material appeared in the 1954 *Handbook* of The Golden State Bull Terrier Club, with the understanding that it would be available for *The Complete Bull Terrier*. And now, back to Miss Montague Johnstone.

The modern Colored Bull Terrier has been evolved from the blending of the Pure White Bull Terrier (with White ancestors going back as far as 1860) and the Staffordshire. The three chief pioneers were Mr. Tunmer, who started blending Staffordshires with Whites around 1907 and remained interested until the early 1930's, Mr. E. A. "Sher" Lyon and Mrs. V. Ellis. Mrs. Ellis is really responsible for my starting in Coloreds. I saw her in the show ring with two red and whites (one of them the important dam, Red Binge) when I had just returned from a last term at school, and remarked on them to Mr. A. J. Harrison, then secretary of the Bull Terrier Club and most kind and helpful. He told me to leave them

191

alone and stick to Whites; so, being perverse, I bet him I'd breed a Colored champion in ten years, and went straight off, that day in the late fall of 1927, to see Mr. Lyon, from whom I bought my first Colored. She was six months old, dark brindle, very light in bone and quite flat-sided. Her head was much more like a Fox Terrier's than like the modern Bull Terrier's, with rose ears, and she had a poor coat. To her credit, she had a lovely little black eye, a perfect mouth, and was the gamest thing on four legs. Her name was Sher Fustian, and directly down from her, by using the best of the White blood without losing the color, emerged Ch. Romany Rhinestone in April 1936. So I had won my bet!

The object then, in those far-off days of 1927, was to attempt to improve heads (which, as we think of them today, just did not exist in the Coloreds) and to get bone and general substance.

Mrs. Ellis, who continually mated Whites to her red and whites, was far more advanced than Mr. Lyon in these respects, but it is to him, above all, that we owe the preservation of the vital color, brindle, in those early days. Mrs. Ellis had, of course, lost this color, but she did get substance, and in Young Woodley had a good headed dog who did well about 1929. In 1930 she bred the outstanding red and white, Hunting Blondi. He won two Challenge Certificates and two Reserve Challenge Certificates, and would undoubtedly have been the first red champion but for his early death at 18 months of age, without having sired a litter. He was by The Sheik of Chartham (pws) ex Little Bella (red), a very great bitch, and a unique and brilliant forecast of the years to come.

The honor of first Colored champion goes to Mr. Dockerill's Ch. Lady Winifred, who won her title in 1931. Brindle and white, by Typical Jim (pws), chiefly Roscolyn blood, ex Princess Ida (br), Gladiator and Sher blood. She carried more than 50% White blood and was outstanding in her day. She was bred from but nothing outstanding came down from her.

Another famous dog of this day was Mrs. Symes' brindle dog, Nelston Cotton, by Caliph Cotton (pws) ex Brindle Reel (Sher blood). He was rarely if ever beaten for best Colored, was very widely used at stud, and his blood is behind almost every Colored pedigree today.

Those were the great names in those days. The general type of the Coloreds was still so far behind the Whites that they could not be compared with them. How, then, was this improved?

Ch. Beshelson Bayshuck (pws), by Ch. Sure Thing ex Fair Charmer of Exford, was in my opinion the fount of greatness, with Ch. Hades Cavalier (pws), by Ch. Hampstead White Hot ex Ardua Phoebe, of equal importance. Bayshuck was whelped in 1928, Cavalier a little earlier.

Bayshuck gave most, I think, as to bone and substance. Cavalier was probably the strongest influence for heads. Mated to Ch. Debonair of Brum (pws), by Ch. Hades Cavalier ex Treviso, Bayshuck produced the famous litter brothers Ch. Ringfire of Blighty and Rubislaw. In 1936, by mating Romany Red Rufus (red), by Romany Radium (br) ex Merely Mary Ann (pws litter sister of Ch. Black Coffee), by Bayshuck, to Romany Retrospect (br), by Romany Radium ex Cylva Cynthia (pws), by Ch. Ringfire of Blighty, by Bayshuck, I got Ch. Romany Rhinestone (red). In this mating, Bayshuck was doubled through his two sons, and Hades Cavalier appears four times, as he is also doubled behind Romany Radium.

If we call Bayshuck and Hades Cavalier the two "headstones," then we will call Rhinestone the first "milestone." In him, we have a concentration of the two "headstones," plus a doubled dose of the original and now much improved Colored blood bred down from Sher Fustian through her son, Romany Ringer (br), who, mated to the challenge certificate winning pws Shelford Sweet Surprise (by Ch. Devil of Doore), produced Romany Rondeau (br), the dam of Romany Radium. Rhinestone, of course, was the result of mating halfbrother and sister, both by Romany Radium.

This doubling of the Colored line strengthened the actual color factor. Romany Radium had one line of unbroken brindle back for ten generations. I checked this with Mr. Lyon at the time, and it is thanks to this concentration of color that Rhinestone proved "whole for color": that is, he never sired a white puppy to any bitch of any color, or to Pure White bred bitches, nor did his son, Ch. Romany Roman (br).

Ch. Romany Rhinestone, a light red and white, was as sensational in his day as Hunting Blondi was in his. He had a tremendous head, very powerful and completely filled, a beautifully placed eye, and very good feet. His bone was almost unbelievable for those days.

193

It is interesting to note that two years later (in 1938) Mr. Oppenheimer doubled Rubislaw by mating his Ch. Cedran White Queen (by Rubislaw) to Ch. Krackton Kavalier (also by Rubislaw) and got his great Ch. Ormandy's Mr. McGuffin as a result. McGuffin also had his immense bone, and just as Rhinestone is the source of great bone in modern Coloreds, so Mr. McGuffin is the source in the modern Whites. This proved beyond doubt, I think, that Bayshuck is the original source of bone.

Rhinestone only sired one champion, Ch. Romany Roman ex a good brindle by Ch. Gardenia Guardsman. Roman's career at stud was blighted by the war, and he is chiefly of interest as being behind the lovely Ch. Charm of Coyney and her sister Romany Rendezvous, who won really well at the small wartime shows, and produced Romany Rateing, who has sired a lot of winners.

It was from his bitches that great things came from Rhinestone. Two litter sisters in particular are of the greatest importance. They were whelped in June 1938, by Rhinestone ex the lovely brindle and white Ch. Jane of Petworth, by Old Jimmy's Double (br) ex Kowhai Chita (pws) and bred by Mr. R. Justice. This litter contained two bitches, Stronghold Lollypop (tricolor) and Stronghold Jeanette (black-brindle). Lollypop was sold to Mrs. Tom Marchant and mated to Borderland Sea Fever (br). Limpsfield Salty Sam (br) ex Limpsfield Lorelei (br) produced a really great little dog in Blue Cross Boy (red). In looks, very much a smaller edition of Rhinestone, he would have been a certain champion but for the war.

A repeat of that mating produced a top class brindle bitch in Blanmerle Sea Poppy (br). Sea Poppy, mated to Brendon Branch (pws by Ch. Radium Brigadier), produced a very good litter containing three or four winners, the most important of which were Blanmerle Beau (br) and Blanmerle Barque (br). Many of the best of the present day winners are descended from these two.

Blanmerle Barque is in the female line behind Ch. Romany Rhinegold, Ch. Romany Rhine Maiden, Ch. Romany Rhine Wine and Ch. Ormandy's Limpsfield Winston. Thus, Blanmerle Sea Poppy, Blanmerle Barque, Limpsfield Conk, Limpsfield Fifinella, who, mated to Ch. Romany Rather Likely (br) (by Ch. Ormandy's Young Lochinvar, pws, ex Romany Rather Lovely), produced the two outstanding litter brothers, Ch. Romany Rhinegold and

Winston, bred by Mrs. M. Molesworth, whose longstanding prefix of "Limpsfield" is much in evidence here.

Blanmerle Beau is chiefly important through his brindle daughter Blanmerle Bowline (ex Coyney Dainty, by Ch. Ormandy's Mr. McGuffin, pws); Bowline, mated to Ch. Romany Reliance, produced two sisters, Ogbourne Impressive (br) and Blanmerle Bettina (br). Impressive, mated to Ch. Ormandy's Kertrim Bosun (pws), produced the Color Bred White Ch. Contango Dimmick Commodore, and Bettina, mated to Ch. The Sphinx (cbw), produced the Color Bred White Ch. Beech House Snow Vision. Snow Vision, mated to Ch. Romany Rite (by Ch. Romany Rather Likely ex Raydium Belinda) produced Ch. Romany Repeat Performance, winner of the Ormandy Jug for 1955, now owned by Mr. and Mrs. James W. Longley, Silver Spring, Maryland, U.S.A. All three, Snow Vision, Repeat Performance, and Commodore, carry brindle, although Snow Vision (with a brindle head mark) is the only one to advertise the fact.

The other sister, Stronghold Jeanette, went to Mrs. "Contango" Schuster, who mated her to a good red in Coulan of Lueuch, and got a brindle bitch called Contango Courtesy. I suggested to Mrs. Schuster that she mate her to Bulak Blackshirt, a good son of the great headed Ch. Gardenia (pws) and she got as a result the key dog Contango Consul (br). Mrs. Schuster then mated Consul back to his own grandmother, Jeanette, and got Contango Cobblestone (br), who had a remarkable head but was undershot.

When Cobblestone was about a year old, I had a magnificent-headed red and white in Northorpe Nonpareil sent down from the North for mating to Ch. Romany Roman. When I saw her, I wired for her owner's permission to use Cobblestone, and got it. Nonpareil was by Old Lane Snow Drift (by Ch. Raydium Brigadier) ex Vintania (by Ch. Velhurst Vindicator). As soon as I was able to do so, I bought these lovely red and white bitches, but was so hampered by the prevailing war conditions that I was unable to do justice to either of them, though Nonpareil did produce a lovely brindle and white bitch to Romany Rambler. We sent her to Ireland and so lost her, but she made a great name for herself over there.

Nonpareil's litter to Cobblestone produced the key bitch Romany Rivet (black-brindle) and another most beautiful red and white

195

bitch that Mrs. Schuster bought and most sadly lost through illness.

Though of entirely different types, both Rivet and her sister would have won their full titles but for the war. Rivet, still in great heart although nearing fourteen years of age, is the cobby type. Her sister was a great big one like her dam.

Rivet, mated during the war to Ormandy Sunny Day (pws) by Ormandy's Mr. McRumpus ex Maginot, produced the *second milestone in Ch. Romany Reliance* (bk-br). In the same litter was Romany Radar (br), who took the reserve challenge certificate behind his brother at the first big postwar show; Romany Resolve, who went to Ireland and became an Irish champion, was a black-brindle bitch, the best of the lot—perhaps the best bitch I've ever seen. I lost her with hardpad at just under a year, and with her lost not only one of the most delightful personalities one could ever wish for, but a source of potential greatness. Radar also died young as a result of illness (during the war and just after it, disease was very prevalent, and the "new" and deadly hardpad, which no one knew how to treat, killed very many dogs). He is chiefly of interest as being behind English and American Ch. Romany Remarkable.

Ch. Romany Reliance sired six champions, two being dogs: Ch. Romany Rough Weather (br) and Ch. Rickmay Retort (bk-br); and four being bitches, Ch. Blanmerle Brindi (br) sister to Ogbourne Impressive and Blanmerle Bettina, Ch. Rougemont Demoisell (bk-br), Ch. Kowhai Rose Revived (br) and Ch. Bliss of Upend (bk-br). Besides these he sired a multitude of winners. Almost every bitch in the country visited him and to almost every bitch he sired a winner. Many people wondered why I had ever parted with him.

During the war, when I could only keep the bare bloodlines going, and those only because good friends took them in for me, I bred very few litters indeed and had to decide which to keep while they were still very young. But for the kindness of Mrs. "Monkery" Holmes, who took Rivet to live with her and whelped her for me, that litter might never have been bred. I had no home of my own at that time.

When the litter was twelve weeks old, I selected the bitch mentioned above, and Radar, who at that age was much the better of the two brothers, and who was the one Mr. Jennings wanted. I would not part with him and sold him Reliance as being the next best of the dog pups. I saw Reliance again at about seven months and still preferred Radar. Then, between seven months and ten months, Reliance produced the most terrific fill-up and downface. He has a head which will perhaps never be surpassed, though there are some who prefer that of his son, Rough Weather. In addition to the outstanding head, Reliance had tremendous bone, beautiful front and feet, and a really wonderful eye. He also had faults: straight stifles and a body that lacked shape. As a sire, he proved most potent, stamping his stock again and again with heads that left the Whites behind, and which twenty years before would only have existed in a breeder's dream. He also reproduced his faults, so, about 1946, we had to look for something else besides heads. We'd got them, fixed and breeding true. Now we had to get shape: good stifles and hocks, sound action, and a better layback of shoulder.

Onto the stage then, as our *third milestone*, comes an elegant red lady in the person of Marle Hill Miniver, by Still Water (br) ex Betty of Thistlewood (tri). She was Miss Williams' pet bitch, and no thought of stardom ever entered her head when Miss Williams joined me immediately after the war with this birthday present she had received a couple of years earlier. Marle Hill Miniver had a long clean head, with nice high eye placement, but without down-face. She was light in bone and rather on the leg, but she had something the others hadn't—beautifully laid back shoulders, a most shapely body and good stifles and hocks. She covered the ground at any speed, smoothly and with grace. She was, in fact, the perfect complement to Reliance. Mated to Reliance in December 1946, Marle Hill Miniver produced a small litter of four pups, one of which was lost. The three reared became Ch. Romany Rough Weather, Romany Rather Lovely (both rich brindle and white) and Romany Rough and Tumble (tri). The last named had several nice litters but persisted in reproducing almost 100% blacks.

The other two in the litter made history.

Rather Lovely had one litter only, to Ch. Ormandy's Young Lochinvar (pws) by Monkery's Banner ex Tom's of Ormandy (pws), whelped in January 1949, and consisting of three brindle and white dogs, one black-brindle dog, and three white bitches, one of which was selected for rearing.

The white bitch, Romany Runner Duck, had one litter to Ch. Romany Rich Reward, which included Romany Runner Beau

197

(cbw), challenge certificate winner at Windsor in 1952. The three brindle dogs became Ch. Romany Rather Likely, Romany Roast Goose, and Romany Rolling Spitfire. Spitfire was sold up north, where he sired a number of winners and did well in the ring until he injured a leg and became permanently unsound. The other two have remained with us.

Rather Likely has sired three champions: the brindle bitch, Ch. Romany Rite, ex Radium Belinda (pws), and two brothers, Ch. Romany Rhinegold and Ch. Ormandy's Limpsfield Winston. Rather Likely is also the sire of the key bitch Romany Rest Cure (fawn) ex Marle Hill Miniver.

Rest Cure had proved herself one of the greatest dams ever. In her first litter, to Reliance, she produced the brindle dog Romany Representative, exported to Italy, now an international champion in Italy, Switzerland, and France, and good enough to have sailed through to his title in this country. In her next, to Ch. Romany Rich Reward, Rest Cure produced Ch. Romany Refreshed, Romany Restored (both silver brindles), African Ch. Romany Rhodesian, and Romany Refresher (U.S.A.).

Romany Roast Goose, sire of many winners, produced two outstanding litters. The first was from Romany Rising Tide (cbw by Rough Weather ex Romany Rainstorm). This litter included Ch. Romany Reprieved (U.S.A.), Rising Tempo (br), and Rising Flame (red). Reprieved sired English and American Ch. Romany Remarkable. Rising Tempo won one challenge certificate and, before being sold, sired Ch. Vestex Vain Lady (red) from his first bitch. Rising Flame has won many major awards in the north. The second outstanding litter by Romany Roast Goose was from Romany Ridge (br), by Rough Weather ex Raydium Roxanna. This litter included American Ch. Romany Ritual, first Colored Bull Terrier ever to go Best in Show, all breeds, in the U.S.A. (she won four such awards), and Romany Runic (br) a dog who went straight to the top in Kenya, and also went Best in Show, all breeds, at Kenya's top yearly event.

Rough Weather, like his ancestor Rhinestone, has shown his greatness chiefly through his daughters, of which two are champions—Highville Lassie (br) and Romany Right as Rain (cbw). It is to his daughters, more than to any other influence, that this kennel has reached the standard so far achieved. We have yet to

198

Eng. Ch. Romany Rhine Wine, whelped 1952, by Ch. Romany Rhinegold ex Ch. Romany Refreshed.

improve hind action; we still get bad mouths, but when we turn up a faded snapshot of little Sher Fustian, and then go outside and look at Rhinegold and Refreshed and their twin daughters playing in the paddocks, we know that twenty-five years have not been wasted.

To sum up, here are the most-important-of-all dogs in the evolution of the modern Colored Bull Terriers, between the years of 1928 and 1954: Ch. Beshelson Bayshuck, Ch. Hades Cavalier, Romany Radium, Ch. Romany Rhinestone, Contango Consul, Romany Rivet with her son Ch. Romany Reliance, Marle Hill Miniver with her son and daughter, Ch. Romany Rough Weather and Romany Rather Lovely, and her most important ancestors, Velhurst Viking, Ch. Velhurst Vindicator, Ch. Raydium Brigadier, Ch. Ormandy's Dancing Time (whose influence is very marked through her grandson Ch. Romany Rich Reward), and Ch. Romany Rather Likely, through his son Ch. Romany Rhinegold. His other son, Ch. Ormandy's Limpsfield Winston, who has so influenced the modern Color Bred Whites for good, will probably appear later behind Colored winners.

It has given me very great pleasure to note that, during the last few years, the Colored Bull Terriers have really been making friends in America. I hope they make many more. And I hope that one day, not too long delayed, they may be considered as they are in England, as one breed with their White brothers, and be judged together in the same ring.

17

Superficial Faults and Their Significance

by Raymond H. Oppenheimer

(Because it so graphically underlines the point we have made of breeding for what one does like, rather than against what one does not like, we include this article from Mr. Oppenheimer's book "After Bar Sinister". This book, and the earlier "McGuffin and Co.", are classic works on the breed that every Bull Terrier enthusiast will want in his library. They are published by The Dog World Ltd., Ashford, Kent, England.)

THE appearance in the ring last year of a dog with a mark on his tail, the award to him of a Challenge Certificate and of a reserve-best-of-sex card and his selection as a competitor for the major Trophies has, as might have been expected, set off a fresh controversy.

As usual those who are most alarmed and excited over the problem are the same sort of people who thirty years ago would have frothed at the mouth over ticks, over a few misplaced teeth, over slightly soft ears or any other of the superficial faults.

Ormandy's Bar Sinister, Winner of the Stud Dog Prize for 1965 and 1966. Not shown because he was a partial unilateral cryptorchid (one testicle normal and fully descended into the scrotum, and the other partially descended), Bar Sinister was otherwise a dog of unparalleled excellence. Bred for his virtues, he produced two Regent Trophy winners, two Ormandy Jug winners, and other toppers.

Ch. Ormandy's Thunderflash, son of Bar Sinister.

The truth of the matter is that pink noses, incorrect mouths, soft ears, light and wall eyes, unilateral cryptorchidism and marks behind the collar are only seven different facets of the same problem, that of the polygenic recessive and how to deal with it.

Events over the years have proved beyond a doubt that a policy which puts a taboo on any single fault is disastrous so far as breed progress is concerned. In fact it is only fair to say that had some of the breeders not been more far-seeing than some of the legislators our breed certainly and many others probably, would be thirty years behind the advanced position it and they have now reached.

An appreciation of this fact is absolutely fundamental to progress, and what is most required of judges is that they shall calmly and dispassionately assess the virtues and the faults of each animal which comes before them, balancing the one against the other. I have said that a variety of shortcomings in our breed are only different facets of the same problem. Let us now examine the lessons of history in this respect and see if they bear out what I have written.

The great Brigadier, when he first appeared in the ring, had an extremely pink nose. The superficialists, in other words those who could not see the wood for the trees, made just the same fuss over his pink nose as has since been made over other similar defects. If they had had their way he would never have won a prize and would therefore scarcely have been used at stud. Yet this pink nose caused no concern whatever in subsequent generations.

Twenty or thirty years earlier, in fact, a dog with such a nose never would have been seen in public.

Let us pass on from there to incorrect mouths. Mrs. Schuster never bothered to show Contango Cobblestone because he was undershot and because in the then climate of opinion he would never have won a prize nor been used at stud except by the percipient breeder. Miss Montague-Johnstone was one of the far-seeing and by using him produced Romany Rivet, dam of Reliance. Miss Weatherill and I never troubled to show Souperlative Soap Bubble because of her mouth. Many people would never have bred from her either for the same reason, magnificent bitch though she was. Had she been discarded there never would have been a Snowflash.

Next let us move on to light and/or wall eyes. The Knave had a light one. The dams of the Sphinx and of Starshine had wall eyes.

What a tragedy it would have been if these three first-class animals had never been used or if the two latter had never been bred!

Before the last war ears such as Princeling's would have condemned him to life as a pet. Yet if he had not been used there would never have been a Barbelle, a Rheingold, a Silver Bob and a dozen others.

Exactly the same principle applies in the case of Bar Sinister, from one of whose normal brothers more unilateral cryptorchids are descended than have come down from Bar Sinister himself.

Over the years I am happy to say a more rational attitude has been adopted toward the first five of these defects with great success and profit to the breed and we must hope that increased knowledge will help the Kennel Club to a more sensible and constructive handling of the testicle problem in due course.

Let us now return in conclusion to the point which started us off, namely to the question of marks behind the collar.

Souperlative Amelia Bebe was a good bitch but she had a black spot on the root of her tail. She was mated and produced the great Spurrell. I cannot, offhand, remember anything by Spurrell nor indeed anything descended from him in the first two or three generations which was marked behind the collar. Yet, in total contrast, I could name at least a dozen animals descended from Ben, of which Tracval's Barney Boy is indeed one, which are marked behind the head. There is no mark behind Ben, known to me anyway, for endless generations, in fact not till we get back into the dim ages with Hampstead Heathen.

What this demonstrates, as do all other similar cases, is that there is no sense whatsoever in refraining from breeding from *really top-class* animals carrying one of these polygenic recessives unless one is able also to avoid using any of their relations since these, even if on the surface unaffected, are very likely to transmit the defect. As this is the case, no good but actual harm is done if first-class animals are debarred from the ring or the prize list while their less good contemporaries can win the highest honors, especially since such a bar encourages faking which soon becomes widespread.

There is, moreover, the basic fact which should never be lost sight of in addition to the foregoing, and that is that for very straightforward genetic reasons a dog with outstanding virtues and outstanding faults is arithmetically more likely to transmit his virtues than his faults, because virtues (in our breed anyway) are in the genetic sense of the term dominant, while faults are recessive. In fact, at the very worst, if one mates together two animals, one of which has one of the defects of which I have written, it could only be even money on it reappearing in the puppies whereas, again at the very worst, it is three to one on such an animal transmitting a virtue. Therefore, those who will not take chances in breeding are always stacking the odds against themselves as compared with breeders who will take chances.

To sum up then, fanciers should maintain an entirely dispassionate attitude to all faults and to all virtues, and breeders, judges and critics alike should bear in mind that the entire problem revolves round a sensible balancing of the faults against the virtues.

The breed standard makes the position extremely clear when it states very plainly and simply that any departure from the list of desired points is a fault and that the seriousness of the fault should be in exact proportion to its degree.

In other words how badly undershot or overshot a mouth is, how soft the ears are, how pink the nose is, how big is the mark behind the collar, how blue or how light is an eye or how abnormal are the testicles has to be balanced by breeder or critic against the virtues of any animal which carries such a fault or faults.

The basic point at issue is quite simply how bad are the points, superficial or indeed anatomical, carried by any animal and how do they compare with his or her virtues. The good judges and the clever breeders will work out the answers to the best advantage and history in the vast majority of cases will support the decisions which they reach.

So many people, who panic over these superficial faults, seem to forget that in breeding for the show ring the object must be the production of outstanding animals. So long as this is achieved, it does not matter how many faults the less-good puppies have from a show point of view, provided always that they are typical, healthy and good tempered.

In order to breed outstanding animals one must use dogs and bitches with outstanding virtues. If these virtues can best be found in animals that have superficial aesthetic faults as well, then they must be used, and by skilful selection the faults discarded in future generations and the virtues retained.

18

Winners from Britain

by Raymond Oppenheimer

THE results of the Bull Terrier Club of America Specialty Show at Chicago in April of this 1968th year of grace reached me at almost the same moment as an invitation from my friend, the Author, to contribute a new chapter to the second edition of his admirable book.

The four top winners in the White variety at Chicago were: Best of Breed, *Ch. Swainshouse Sportsman,* bred by W. Peace and owned by Charles and Susan Meller; Best of Opposite Sex, *Ch. Meltdown Mark,* bred by Mrs. M. Treen and owned by Oliver W. Ford; Winners Bitch and Best of Winners, *Sturdee Wilsmere Christabelle,* bred by Mrs. E. Ruse and owned by Mr. and Mrs. Wm. W. Colket; and Winners Dog, *Silverwood Monkery's Caviar,* bred by Mrs. P. E. Holmes and owned by Monroe McIntyre. There were 27 in competition, and the judge was Dr. Harry L. Otis.

Since all four were bred in Britain, and all are by stud dogs at Ormandy, I thought readers might find it of interest to know some of the background to these winners.

Generally speaking, for obvious reasons, dogs in any breed tend to have a more widespread influence than bitches, except insofar as

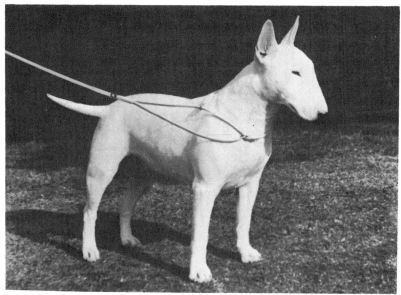

Ch. Phidgity Snow Dream

Ch. Souperlative Summer Queen

the dam of an influential dog may be said to have an influence through him. This, indeed, had been the position in Bull Terriers until twelve years ago, when two bitches appeared that in combination were to revolutionize the breed. Moreover, the two were first cousins, though of utterly contrasting types.

The elder, by nearly a year, was CH. PHIDGITY SNOW DREAM. Bred by Miss L. Graham-Weall, Snow Dream was by Ch. Ormandy Souperlative Snowflash (Bradbourne's Prince Regent ex Souperlative Soap Bubble) ex Phidgity Shepherdess (Ch. Ormandy's Limpsfield Winston ex Ormandy's Corky). She was a very small, absolutely exquisite, specimen with a tremendous downface, a very short back, a great spring of rib and sound—certainly the best bitch any of us had seen up to then.

A year later, her cousin CH. SOUPERLATIVE SUMMER QUEEN arrived. Bred by Mr. H. Langford, Summer Queen was by Ch. Beechhouse Snow Vision ex Souperlative Spring Song (a litter sister of Snowflash).

It would be difficult to imagine two animals in the same breed more of a contrast than Snow Dream and Summer Queen. The latter would comfortably have made two of her cousin, but each was a perfect complement to the other. Summer Queen had the size, the power, and a most wonderful placid temperament which she inherited from her sire, and to which the present good-humored winners owe a great deal.

In due course, Snow Dream produced Ch. Phidgity Phlasher of Lenster (by Snow Vision) and Ch. Romany Romantic Vision (by Ch. Romany Robin Goodfellow).

Summer Queen, mated to Phlasher, gave us Chs. Ormandy Souperlative Chunky, Ormandy Souperlative Princeling and Souperlative Brinhead. Princeling in turn is the sire of Ch. Ormandy's Ben of Highthorpe, and Brinhead is the sire of Ormandy Souperlative Bar Sinister and Ch. Souperlative Masta Plasta of Ormandy.

Summer Queen, next mated to Romantic Vision, gave us Ch. Souperlative Sunshine, dam of Bar Sinister and of Masta Plasta.

Having recorded this, let us turn back now and look at our four Chicago winners once more, from a pedigree point of view.

Best of Breed SPORTSMAN is by Masta Plasta out of a granddaughter of Phlasher and of Snowflash.

Ch. Phidgity Shepherdess

Ch. Beechhouse Snow Vision

Ch. Souperlative Masta Plasta of Ormandy

Ch. Phidgity Phlasher of Lenster

Ch. Romany Romantic Vision

Souperlative Spring Song

Ch. Ormandy Souperlative Princeling

Ch. Ormandy's Ben of Highthorpe

Ch. Souperlative Brinhead

Best of Opposite Sex MARK is by Ben, ex a daughter of Princeling.

Winners Dog CAVIAR is by Bar Sinister out of a daughter of Ben which is out of a daughter of Princeling. Winners Bitch CHRISTABELLE is by Thunderflash, son of Bar Sinister, out of a granddaughter of Snow Vision.

I doubt that the four top winners at any show before have ever been so closely related, or too, that their parents have been. The motto of all this seems to me that inbreeding, wisely conducted, brings great benefits. But I've said all that before, haven't I?

However, I think that it is worth repeating once more because, for two different reasons, many breeders in the United States (at least viewed from a distance) seem to avoid it. The first reason is the factual one that often a suitable dog is not easily available. The second is that they seem to be afraid to do it.

There is, however, nothing of which to be afraid as long as one observes three cardinal principles:

1. Do not get too many crosses of dangerous dogs, genetically speaking, close up in the pedigree.
2. Do not inbreed with ill-suited mates. (I use ill-suited here in reference to type.)
3. Never use second-class dogs.

One final point, in a positive sense. My personal experience has led me to believe that while all forms of intelligent inbreeding can bring great rewards, a very successful form of it is to mate together the grandsons and granddaughters of a great dog. This method has produced some of the most influential results in our breed's history.

19

The Miniature Bull Terrier

SINCE 1963, the American Kennel Club has included the Miniature Bull Terrier among the breeds that may be entered in the Miscellaneous Class at licensed and member AKC shows, and at Obedience Trials. (Entries in the Miscellaneous class compete for Best Dog in Miscellaneous Class or Best Bitch in Miscellaneous Class, and are not eligible for further inter-breed competition at the show.)

In the history and "summary" which the American Kennel Club provides as a guide to these breeds, it states as the aim of breeders "a down-faced smaller dog, weighing about 16 pounds, and identical in make and shape and every single feature with the full-sized Bull Terrier." The specifications for size read: "To 14 inches inclusive. Weight not to exceed 20 pounds."

For the first edition of this book, Mrs. M. C. P. Simpson, whose Solway Kennels in England did much to develop and popularize the Miniature Bull Terrier, provided us with the following background on the Variety:

> THE MINIATURE Bull Terrier is the "Pocket Edition" of the Standard, the desired points being the same but the height may not exceed fourteen inches at the shoulder.

211

A historic picture of Miss Catherine Cameron and Mrs. Arthur Burden exhibiting two Toy Bull Terriers, Grassmere Nell and Grassmere Atom, at the Ladies Kennel Association show in Long Island in 1913.

Eng. Ch. Solway Navigation Surprise, height 13¾", weight 22 lbs.

Ch. Oldlane Highburn Selby, whelped 1952.

Eng. Ch. Fury of Upend, whelped **1951.**

Eng. Ch. Navigation Billy Boy, whelped 1954. Winner of six Certificates, including Crufts 1955 and 1956.

From the records in the nineteenth century when the name "Bull Terrier" was first used, it seems there were always small specimens of the breed of 14 to 25 pounds weight and it is from these small Bull Terriers that the modern Miniatures have evolved. They conjure memories of the Georgian Epoch in this country, when these game little ones were used in the rat pits and sums of money were wagered on them. Their courage was wonderful and a dog that gave in would have been a disgrace to his breed and probably to his owner. These small Bull Terriers were crossed with the White English Terrier, now extinct, and it is from this strain that the modern Miniatures are sprung and from them they derive their stamina and courage.

Until 1918 the Bull Terrier Club encouraged the breeding of both Bull Terriers in Standard sizes and Miniature Bull Terriers, but then the promotion of Miniatures was no longer among their objectives, although they put on classes for them at their Club shows. These were limited by weight of 12 pounds maximum and no Challenge Certificates were offered.

In 1938 Colonel Glyn founded the Miniature Bull Terrier Club and the breed was recognized by the Kennel Club as a variety of Bull Terrier which must be measured as not exceeding 14 inches at shoulder, and the Kennel Club offered six Challenge Certificates a year. With a height of 14 inches, this means weights of about 18 to 25 pounds, though no weight is given in the Standard.

At that period (with a few exceptions) there were few really good specimens that looked like Bull Terriers. For the most part they were apple-headed, snipey-nosed and light in bone—but many Miniatures were mated to small sized Bull Terriers, and the breed improved in appearance and bone.

Puppies bred from one registered Miniature and one Standard Bull Terrier must be registered at the Kennel Club as interbred. If such an interbred be mated to a registered Miniature, the puppies must again be registered as interbred (second generation). If one of this second generation is crossed with a registered Miniature (third generation), the progeny is eligible for registration as Miniature Bull Terriers.

The first Miniature champion was made in 1948; she was Deldon Delovely, white and brindle marked, weight about eighteen pounds, bred by Miss Scott and owned by Mrs. Adlam. The first male champion was Morsley Model, a brindle, twelve and a half inches high, owned and bred by Mr. Stanley North.

Today the breed is growing in popularity and one can really say

Hi Seas Silver Mist, 10 inches. Whelped 1967.

that the dogs being exhibited are Bull Terriers in miniature. As the better specimens appear, the breed will continue to improve and I am quite convinced that given time they will be as good as the Standard, provided the breeders will only breed from the best specimens and introduce new blood by interbreeding with small sized Standard Bull Terriers. These little dogs make ideal house pets, are easy whelpers and devoted mothers and have the courageous and true Bull Terrier character. Special classes are provided and they never compete against the Standard.

One of the chief problems which confronts Miniature breeders is the variety of size in a litter. Some really good specimens grow over 14 inches and cannot be exhibited, while others in the litter remain too small, being almost Toys and not exceeding eight pounds in weight when fully grown. These latter lack Bull Terrier type and have snipey noses and large eyes. Having bred Miniatures for twenty years, I cannot recall ever having had a really uniform litter, but they have all produced true Bull Terrier coats and, unlike the Standards, seldom have weak stifles or bad action.

Toys and Miniatures in the United States

In the United States, the Toy Variety had some vogue but its death knell was sounded in 1916 when the American Kennel Club ruled that Winners' Classes would not be provided "until such time as the number exhibited shall demonstrate that they should logically be entitled to such classes." Other breeds coming under this ruling at that time included White English Terriers, Bedlingtons, Boxers, etc. 1922 was the year that the last Toy Bull Terrier (under 12 pounds) was exhibited at Westminster.

This maximum weight of 12 pounds for Toys seems to have had some historical basis, as this is the maximum weight given for the variety in the Standard of the Bull Terrier Club of Scotland (1904).

Further evidence is given to this point in the article on "The Toy

Ch. Harpers Toy Soldier, Best of Breed and fifth in Group at Crufts at only nine months of age. Whelped 1962.

Freesail Simone, Miniature, whelped 1960. By Eng. Ch. Navigation Billy Boy ex Freesail Martine. Breeder, L. G. Pepper. Owner, Mrs. Ralph Gordon.

Navigation Tony, tricolor. Height 12 inches, weight 10 lbs.

Navigation Pinto, whelped 1959. Breeder, A. M. Burton. Owner, Mrs. Ralph Gordon.

Bull Terrier," given in Cassell's *New Book of the Dog* (1907), written by Lady Everland Ewart: "The most valuable Toy Bull Terriers are small and very light in weight, and these small dogs usually have apple heads.

"In drawing up a show schedule of classes for the breed, it is perhaps better to limit the weight of competitors to twelve pounds. The Bull Terrier Club booked fifteen pounds as the lowest weight allowed of the large breed, and it seems a pity to have an inter-regnum between the large and miniature varieties, still in the interest of the small valuable specimens, this seems inevitable."

Pony Queen, the former property of Sir Raymond Ryrwhitt Wilson, weighed under three pounds.

The difficulties in breeding the Toy Variety around the turn of the century were pretty much the same as those mentioned by Mrs. Simpson. W. J. Pegg, writing in the *Kennel Encyclopaedia* (London, 1907), states:

> Miniature or Toy Bull Terriers which scale in at ten pounds are a miniature edition of the larger variety, their points are exactly the same as those of the larger variety.
>
> Unfortunately, great difficulty is experienced in breeding the Toy Variety with the small 'slit' eye; most of the dogs have prominent 'goggle" eyes. And Toys, generally, lack the finish and filled up muzzle of their larger brothers.

The last exhibit at Westminster of what might be classed as Miniatures was in 1928. The new impetus for the Variety began in May, 1961, when Mrs. Ralph Gordon imported Ch. Navigation Pinto, brindle and white, and Freesail Simone, fawn and white. Following upon the admission of the Miniatures to the Miscellaneous class in 1963, a Miniature Bull Terrier Club was formed in 1966.

While most of the Miniature Bull Terriers have been of Colored variety, there have been some notable Whites. English Ch. Harper's Toy Soldier of Lenster won at Crufts in 1963, and placed in the Group, beating Standard Bull Terriers among others.

There seems to be a distinct desire in the United States for the small-sized Bull Terrier as he is easier to handle as a pet than his larger brother. I personally know of two occasions on which $1,000 was offered for bitches of 25 pounds or less—and refused.

20

What We Hope For
When We Import from England

(From an article written by the author for the Bull Terrier Annual.)

My good friend Tom Horner asked me as an American to answer the question, "What we hope for when we import from England." As, to put it mildly, we merely hope for an import that will cause all our competitors to die from sheer frustration and envy, it might be better to rephrase the question to, "What we want and what we need when we import from England."

I imagine that most dogs sold for export at a high price are bought more because of their show winnings and the splash they are expected to make over here than because of their ability to produce quality stock. Or, to put it another way, it is not a dog which is bought but a machine to manufacture those beautiful rosettes that the judge hands out to the sound of enthusiastic applause.

With that quite mundane thought in mind, let us analyse the kind of a dog most likely to win over here, remembering that he

The two winners at a Sanction Show of the Bull Terrier Club, London, 1955. Mrs. Ernest Eberhard, judge. Left, Agate's White Knight, Best of Breed, bred and owned by Mrs. M. O. Sweeten. Right, Best Bitch, Two Seater of Tartary, bred by T. Horner, and owned by Mr. and Mrs. F. Bram.

Mrs. Eberhard presents trophy for Best of Breed at Northern Provincial Bull Terriers Championship Show in England, judged by Mr. Eberhard. The winner, Bunty Pride of Kearby (later Ch.), owned by Mr. and Mrs. J. N. Gott.

must be capable of holding his own in competition with the top Terriers of other breeds.

First, if he is to do anything at all in top competition, he must have a good bite. An undershot dog or one with several crooked teeth has three strikes on him to start with. He may win his championship, but he will never do much in the Terrier Group where competition is necessarily based on physical soundness as well as on type. Over here, a poor bite in a Terrier is considered to be a very bad fault indeed.

Second, he must move well both coming and going. Most of those who judge Bull Terriers over here are not breed judges—they generally do at least all Terriers, and quite often all breeds. A dog who swings badly in back or who moves with a stiff-legged action has two strikes against it.

Third, the dog should be well-balanced and of good type, ears on top of his head, alert, a good showman.

That, actually, is what we *want* (with reasonable expectation of being able to get it)—a good dog able to hold his own in the Terrier Group. And that doesn't mean just a nice, sound white dog. It means a dog who can win under breed judges, too, even though we only have a handful of them. The dog must have type, but not at the expense of reasonable soundness.

What we *need* is something else again. Primarily we need breeding stock of the highest type that can produce with a minimum of faults. We do not have the facilities to use a great-headed dog with a bad bite and a poor rear end. The bitches with which he would be used would be an outcross and there would be a far greater likelihood of our picking up his faults than of getting his virtues. At present, one import is cursing us with an unusually high percentage of bad mouths; we are quite bewildered as to how to hold his high type and yet get rid of the bad mouths. We do not have enough stock with his high quality to use and to juggle around until we have the virtues without the faults. In that respect we are in a far different position than you are in England, as you have the facilities to take great type accompanied by considerable unsoundness and to conduct a breeding program that offers a fair chance to hold the type and get rid of the unsoundness.

It is my belief that despite our paucity of top producing stock, we now have enough fundamentally to do a fairly good job of breeding top quality if we can only forget some of the things we don't like and use the dog we really should use in order to get a particular job done. No dog is perfect and we may have to put up with a seldom encountered fault in order to get rid of a common one. It is all a matter of careful study leading up to the best selection.

Our importations in bitches have been lamentably few, which indicates that the studs who come over here are sadly handicapped by generally being presented with outcrosses. For some strange reason, we do not incline towards buying a very good bitch in whelp to a suitable stud plus a reasonably good stud, which would go well with the bitch and her progeny. Perhaps it is because we are not buying a dog but the rosettes it is expected to win for our everlasting glory and satisfaction. It is so much quicker and easier to buy a good one than it is to breed one—and a lot cheaper too. I shudder when I think what our last litter cost us, even though one of the males topped the breed at Westminster.

I think it fairly safe to say that due to the newer imports, the general level of quality is on a sounder basis, and we have a more promising future than we had three or four years ago. We are on the up grade and, given some reasonably good luck, should see an occasional American-bred knocking off our best imports.

But what we do need, and need badly, are top producing studs and dams on which we can depend to give us good mouths and good rears as well as good heads and good type. It would be far better for us if, instead of letting us buy a dog of top quality, you would make a strong effort to sell us a package deal of a well-bred bitch in whelp plus a suitable stud. You have plenty of excellent stock for that purpose, as I saw myself when judging the Northern Provincial Bull Terrier Club Championship show last year and it is a great pity we cannot take full advantage of such dogs. Perhaps some day artificial insemination may become perfected so that we will be able to tap the top producers.

Rhodesian Champion Souperlative Snow White, a Bar Sinister sister, an important influence in development of the breed in South Africa.

Australian Champion Sterling Storm, whelped 1963. Twice Best in Show at the Bull Terrier Club of Australia Championship Show, and top point scoring Bull Terrier for 1964 and 1965. Retired to stud, he sired 1968 Best in Show winner. Owned by Cyril Lee, Merrylands. N.S.W.

Australian Ch. Louisa of Lenster (imp. U.K.) By Am. & Can. Ch. Rombus Astronaut of Lenster ex Lucky Swop of Lenster.

Abraxas Acclimation, young import from England, owned by Monomay Kennels of Campsie, N.S.W., the oldest and longest established Bull Terrier Kennels in Australia—first registered in 1918, but breeders since 1905.

Ch. Kramlla Kommando, at 15 months. Owned by the Kramlla Kennels of Capt. and Mrs. J. Allmark in Victoria, Australia, who brought their foundation stock with them from England 17 years ago.

This month old youngster shows a beautiful clean head, well-placed eyes, and good bone and feet. The nose is just starting to blacken up. (Bull Terrier puppies are usually whelped with all-pink noses, and pink streaks may remain for months.)

This puppy has an unusually good chest, heavy round bone, excellent conformation throughout. But his eyes are not well placed, fill seems a bit lacking, and the chances are that he will not develop into good show type.

A young puppy, about two months old, bred by Miss D. Montague Johnstone. Note the fill, strength of jaw, the good bone and feet, the well-bent stifle, and good back line. A puppy like this would be a very good gamble indeed.

21

How to Pick a Good Bull Terrier Puppy

SOME strains reach their promise early and hold it. Others hold much promise but deteriorate quickly. Still others show little if any early promise but mature into great quality. It is extremely difficult to forecast the show qualities of the mature dog.

I recall a truly great dog—Ch. Ormandy Souperlative Spurrell, an Ormandy Jug winner. This dog was sold as a pet by no less an authority than the Ormandy Kennels but good fortune brought it back into their hands. Ch. Dulac Heathland's Commander was likewise sold as a pet, but fortunately was recovered. Many a time the greatest authorities in the breed have let an unlikely prospect go, only to discover later that a sad mistake had been made.

Sometimes true greatness can be recognized while the puppy is still wet, but even to pick the best in the litter is at best an educated gamble. Bull Terriers grow in sections. The ears usually grow first. Usually the big ear will stop growing long before the rest of the dog does, and so the body which continues to grow will catch up.

Sometimes a body will grow faster than the legs, so that a puppy may be close to a year old before legs and body come into proportion. The top piece may grow faster than the under-jaw so that the puppy at three or four months is painfully overshot—only to develop an even bite when the second teeth come in. The same way hold true of an undershot mouth, as the underjaw may grow faster for a time than does the upper jaw, but eventually the two may come into proportion. However, for show purposes an undershot mouth in a puppy is to be regarded with suspicion. Eyes may be of a poor shape and size, only to take a delightful form when the fill develops. Pure white coats may become ticked at about six or seven months, but in many cases the ticks will disappear before the puppy is a year old.

Even on size, selection is all a gamble. Some puppies may stop growing at six months and weigh the same then as they do at two years. Others will continue to grow and put on weight for 18 months or more, so that the dog that is the smallest in the litter at four or five months may mature larger than its littermates.

Obviously, there are many intangibles at which one can only hazard an educated guess even though one may be thoroughly familiar with the genetic shadow of the parents and grandparents. However, there are certain basic factors that will help to make the guess a bit more certain. For example, there is the structure of the dog: Are his shoulders good? Are his ears well shaped and properly placed on top of his head? Is his eye dark, with no suspicion of a blue spot? Has he a good underjaw, an overshot bite and a strong muzzle, with good profile, and ample bone in front of the eyes? Is his tail set low? When he stands, does he seem to be all in one piece? Even though he may be full of puppy looseness, does he seem to move with a fair degree of certainty? Are his feet tight with thick pads, his bone good? Has his skin the pinkish tinge of health and does his coat have a gloss? Does he look quality? Some puppies look right, others just don't, although one can easily be fooled either way—and the best authorities do get fooled.

If the puppy is to be bought as a pet, probably the safest way to make a purchase is to select a reputable kennel where the dogs appear to be happy, friendly, well fed, and well cared for. A look at the mother can tell much about health and disposition, and much can also be learned from the sire. If the preliminary examination of the way the dogs are kept seems to be satisfactory and the breeding

Eng. Ch. Ormandy Souperlative Spurrell at 10 months. Regent Trophy
winner 1955.

stock is of good quality, then probably the best thing to do is to pick the puppy that first prances happily over to you—in brief, let the puppy do the picking.

As a pet, probably the best age at which to buy is between two and eight months. Sometimes an older dog who has been neglected, and who is pining for companionship, will be the best selection. Such a dog can be recognized almost at a glance because of his apparent hungriness for affection.

If the puppy is old enough, it should have had its permanent shots against distemper and hepatitis. If it is not old enough to have had permanent shots, then it should not be taken until it has had a temporary shot. The puppy should be free of worms, and the breeder should be willing to give a written guarantee as to its health.

Immediately after purchasing a dog, the buyer should take it to a veterinarian for a complete check up. A sick puppy taken into one's home can mean nothing but heartaches, for even if it survives the puppy may be ailing for the rest of its life.

The purchase of a puppy from a reputable breeder and at a fair price is the cheapest purchase in the long run. It costs real money to feed the bitch and the young puppies properly, but prenatal and early care will pay off in future health and well being. It costs at least $75 to raise each one of the average litter of Bull Terrier puppies to two months of age; averaging five to the litter, this means a cash outlay of $375 to $500, exclusive of overhead. There-fore, a price of $125 or $150 for a two- or three-months-old puppy is by no means out of line.

If the puppy is being bought as a pet and also for show or breed-ing, then it should be at least six months old. By that time one can

225

make a good guess as to whether or not the bite will be proper, the form and placement of the eye is taking shape, and the overall contour of the animal can be guessed at rather accurately. To be entirely safe, the puppy should be at least nine or ten months old, as by that time pretty nearly all the gamble will have been taken out of the purchase.

If the puppy is to be bought primarily for breeding or show, then it is better to buy a mature dog from winning lines, one which has been tested in the show ring, and which has produced a litter so that you have proof of fertility. Likewise, when buying for breeding or show, the purchase should be made only after a study of the winning lines in the pedigree. Lines which win mainly against kennel mates should be regarded with suspicion. Those which win consistently at shows such as Westminster can be regarded with greater confidence. The sire that not only wins at the big shows but also places fairly consistently in the Group, and that produces stock which can do likewise, probably represents the best winning line to tap; one of his offspring should be a fairly good gamble if it comes from a suitable bitch.

If you intend to breed dogs, do not bother with your own stud until you are well established. For a small breeder to own a stud is likely to be an extravagance and a handicap to quality breeding. More than one kennel has been ruined by purchasing a stud and using it with all its bitches, suitable or not. If one does not own a stud, then one is not led into temptation but has the choice of all the studs in the country and can make far more rapid progress than if confined to one stud for reasons of pride or economy.

It is best to stake one's "all" on the best bitch that can be bought or imported. The bitch should be purchased only after a study of its pedigree and also after consideration as to which producing stud it can be mated to. Otherwise, one may find himself with a splendid bitch and nothing with which to mate it properly.

Pick particularly the bitch which has a head with plenty of fill, a good profile, well-placed and well-shaped eyes, a good underjaw, erect ears set on top of the head, a good coat, low-set tail, and, along with those essentials, as much soundness as possible. It is better to have a bitch too low and broad than too high and narrow—it is easy to breed the shelly, leggy ones, but almighty hard to breed the ones with substance and of proper station. Avoid like the plague the

Eng. Ch. Tartary Kilsac Brumas, left as a puppy, and right as an adult.

long-headed bitch which falls away under and before the eyes, and which, although pretty, is shelly and leggy.

In follow-up to our own observations on the subject we include a symposium that appeared in the Spring 1968 Bull Terrier Club Bulletin (England). Our thanks to the Honorary Editor of the Bulletin, Mrs. M. O. Sweeten, for her cooperation in this.

It all started with the dilemma of an enthusiastic young man who had come to Britain to buy a first-rate bitch in whelp and subsequently export it to his home. He went to shows, visited kennels, and in fact took far more trouble to educate his eye for a good dog, and to learn the points of the breed, than the majority of people with opportunity on their doorstep. In his wisdom, he realized that he had only broken the surface. In desperation, he asked, "I have this good bitch. When she has her puppies, how on earth am I to tell which one to keep? I haven't the facilities to keep the lot. I've got to sell all but two at about eight weeks. It's all very well for you, you have help and advice, but I must do it alone." I put the question to several prominent breeders, all of whom said there was no sure system, but agreed to make suggestions.

Miss E. Weatherill (*Souperlative*):

What a question! I think ours is just about the most difficult breed in the world from which to select with any certainty a future winner at say eight to ten weeks. One certainly cannot attempt to do so before that time.

I will assume that the breeder having been in possession of the dam since puppyhood has studied the breed standard and will know the salient points to look for. They should bear in mind very carefully that, whilst in this breed good heads are of great importance, there is also, to quote an old friend of mine, "two ends and a middle piece."

I always watch a litter as a whole and see if any one puppy strikes me as outstandingly good more often than the others. I would advise the selector to stand a little way off from the puppies and quietly watch them at play, then separate the sexes, taking the bitches first. One cannot see puppies properly when they are clambering about one's feet. Bitches should be looked at first because dogs are as a general rule larger and more sturdily bilt and the bitches, even the heavy ones, can look on the fine side if examined after the dogs.

Good points to look for are front legs straight, strong; strong toenails, good thick pads to the feet, which should turn neither in nor outwards, and elbows tucked well into the side of the body. Hindquarters well rounded and strong, hocks straight, neither badly turned inwards nor outwards (but allow for a bit of growing weakness here). The expression "cow hocks" means the hock joints turn inwards and the hind feet splay outwards. Some puppies can and do grow out of these, but it is better to avoid them if possible. Back short and strong and absolutely level; they can't grow out of long, weak, dippy backs. Neck of reasonable length and should hold the head up proudly. Head at this age should be rather square, the foreface longer, but not a lot than the forehead, the eyes being set closer to the ears than to the nose. Eyes should be as near black as possible and so should the nose. Ears fairly close set and of thin texture. Mouth—teeth should be correct at this age. Coat dense and milky white, body skin fine and supple to touch when taken between the fingers—it should feel like a soft kid glove and should fit the body tightly.

Faults to try and avoid: A very shy one, they may or may not grow out of this and are useless as show dogs. Bad feeders are also a liability. Very light boned puppies, with narrow bodies and long thin heads and long thin feet. Very common ones and very bad fronted or excessively cow-hocked ones and badly undershot jaws.

It will be appreciated that one looks for certain points in special strains, but here one can only generalize. If the breeder selects a good, solid puppy which looks "square" as a whole—head and body, he has a fair chance of keeping at least a decent one. The head may not be a sensational one on maturity, but at least the puppy should be well built and well balanced. If it is a bitch, then he can apply himself to using the best headed dog of her blood line when he decides to mate her.

Miss L. Graham Weall (*Phidgity*):

The five "experts" stood round the puppy pen gazing at the litter. Two of the party owned the stud dog, had seen numerous litters sired by him, two owned the dam who had had a previous litter, and the last person had seen puppies grow up from this very strain. "I find it very difficult to pick between Betsy and Harry, I think they are extremely promising puppies and I would suggest that you run them both on." "Yes," I agree, "the other two are quite nice, and little Tom is the one that we can safely sell as a pet." "Oh yes" agree the whole party, and dismissing little Tom they all walk away and take a cup of tea.

Needless to remark, Betsy and Harry turned into very nice show dogs, one became a Champion after a slight struggle and the other won a lot of prizes. Little Tom, however, became a real "smasher," was shown three times to become a Champion, won all the Trophies and later won several Best in Shows, much to the delight of his owners who bought him as a pet!

In my opinion, it is impossible to pick the best of a litter as a Novice with no help at all. It is extremely difficult even with the best brains in the dog world, but should I ever have to pick one on my own, I should go for the one with a fearless temperament, the one that is best built (and this you can see even at six weeks) and the one with a wide, strong head and muzzle and hope that it would turn into a downface with no stop.

There is no other breed that alters so much as ours, the really ugly heads so often "come up" and even those with a big eye seem to get a smaller eye as they grow. A short backed puppy will never grow into a long backed dog, and vice versa, but a slightly cow hocked puppy will improve as he grows and very often end up all right behind, provided he has a well turned stifle.

Perhaps one of the most interesting parts of breeding Bull Terriers is the fact that they are so difficult. So if you are lucky and get your "flyer" in your first litter, good luck to you. If you don't, just go on trying. It is well worth it.

Mrs. P. Holmes (*Monkery*):

There are no hard and fast rules when it comes to picking the best puppy in a litter. As an example—a very fine fox terrier-like head on a six weeks puppy from my bitch will undoubtedly strengthen, while in a litter of different breeding such a head will finish up looking like a Borzoi. So don't be in a hurry to select your puppy, particularly if you don't know the line. It will simplify things a lot if you decide you want a dog or a bitch from this particular mating.

Take note of the puppies' heads as they are born and while they are still wet, as at this moment you can get a fair idea of how they will look eventually. At three weeks take another good look. They should be fat and square and heads should have a smooth look— very strong above the eyes and nice bumps below them. It is unlikely they will have any profile, but I do like to see what I call a good top to the head and a hint of a Roman finish. At six weeks a lot of puppies go plain as their faces lengthen, though I must say that a really outstanding one in my lot is never plain at any age.

I don't consider that structural faults really show themselves in earnest until the puppies are eight weeks. As you have decided to keep a bitch, you must now sell the dogs and really concentrate on the bitches. Although you can't be sure of temperaments until about five months, notice how they react to strangers. Don't keep a shy one, however beautiful, she can look like Helen of Troy at home and utterly destroy herself by being frightened in the show ring. What about fronts? Don't discard an otherwise promising puppy if she has a rather loose or slightly crooked front, as this can

230

be improved out of all knowledge by half-an-hour's walk on the road EVERY day when old enough. Get someone to walk away from you with the puppies following and watch how they move behind. As the number of good movers in our breed can be counted on the fingers of one hand, the odds are against them. Ideally, the hind feet should move straight forward tracking the front ones— more likely they will,

(a) be cow hocked (hocks turned in and feet turned out). This often improves with lots of free galloping.
(b) move straight, but with the feet too close and in some cases almost brushing each other. A lot move like this and it is not as bad as
(c) a swinging action with feet practically crossing. This never improves much and unless the puppy is otherwise a flyer, discard it.

The heads should now be making a move, although some don't really start to come before ten to twelve weeks. Personally, I should expect a downface at ten weeks and the foreface to be filling up and strengthening. If still plain at fifteen weeks, let her go, as these days a good head is a must.

The next thing to worry about is how they are going to teethe and until this is safely accomplished, you can't make your final choice. Quite an alarming number of Bull Terriers have slightly faulty mouths and if one of the puppies is really undershot, don't keep it. Sometimes the first teeth are wrong, but this can be ignored, as often the second ones come through perfectly alright.

Now you can make your final choice and if you have been lucky, you will have a well made puppy—square, strong and bold, with a good head, a reasonably good mover and ready now for the serious work of becoming a STAR.

Mrs. J. Schuster (*Contango*):

Not a very easy subject, I feel, as some people have an eye for a dog and others have not. However, once you have decided on which Stud Dog to use for your bitch, try and see as many litters by that dog as you can. This may not always be easy, as most breeders do not allow complete strangers to see their puppies until they have been covered against infection. I don't think our breed is one of the

231

easiest to pick, as the types of head in various sires vary considerably at an early age, some being filled right up at birth and others showing no outstanding profile, yet finish with a screaming down-face!

I do like to see a head well filled on top of the skull, even if dipping a bit between the eyes, so long as there is a pronounced turn down to nose or "Parrot" finish. This usually finishes a very good head, at least I have found this with my bitches. I have a quick look at each pup as soon as it is born—held in profile the head at that moment shows the "shape of things to come," yet a few hours later the line has gone. A small mark of something like Gentian Violet (lipstick will do if nothing else) put on the pups will help you to remember your first choice, if you get confused with a litter of whites. Personally, I always find one's eye always seems to go to a certain pup when coming up to the box, and sure enough it's the one you first thought of.

Mistakes are often made even by experts and nothing is more maddening than to have sold a nice pet puppy and see it nine months later grown into a "flyer" and the owners won't show it.

I have only mentioned the head line but as the pups get on their legs conformation—shortness of back, front, bone, expression, ear, carriage, etc., must all be considered, so I do think the best thing is to try and get an experienced breeder to give your pups a "Look-over" for you.

Mrs. M. O. Sweeten (*Agates*):

I do not expect to get a really top class puppy in every litter and champions are rarer still, but there are usually one or more puppies in each litter which are of considerably higher quality than the others. Bearing this sobering thought in mind, it is quite certain that they won't all be champions! The litter that is so even that "they are as like as peas in a pod" may be very nice, but it is unlikely to contain anything exceptional. It is the puppy which is different from the others which may well be very, very good (or very, very bad!) And whether it is to be good or bad is something that you can get to know by studying your own bitch line and seeing as many progeny of the stud dog as you can.

Newly born puppies show quite a lot of differentiation while they

Berryborn Harvester, above as a 6-
weeks puppy, and left as an adult, but
before being shown.

are still wet and an outstanding head will often be apparent at this
stage, but after a short time, perhaps two hours, a healthy litter will
be warm and filled and the head shapes can no longer be distinguished, although a truly exceptional head may stand out. When
the puppies are on their feet, I look for the puppy which stands all
square and seems solid and compact, with a filled deep head. Very
soon, the dogs must be considered apart from the bitches, as they
are often bigger and heavier.

I spend hours just looking at the litter, not looking for anything
in particular, just looking. Every time I find that a puppy catches
my eye, I pick it up and put a mark under its tummy (nail varnish
is best), then return the pup to the litter. Whenever I watch them,
I repeat the process and I find that time and time again, it is the
same puppy that catches my eye. That then is my No. 1 choice.

I never "run on" a puppy alone, they thrive much better with
company and I would always discount the very fine puppy—if it is
fine in babyhood, it will certainly not be a real bull terrier packed
with substance. I would not keep a puppy that was cow hocked or
badly out at elbow, nor would I keep one that was very long in
back. I would expect the puppy of my choice to be solid and square
with a filled strong head with Roman finish and plenty of bone
below the eye. As the puppy grows and reaches 4–6 months, the
finer points can be assessed, but there is many a hazard between
eight weeks and the show ring and, as Mrs. Adlam said to the young
Raymond Oppenheimer many years ago, "they change so dear."

"Wildfire" receiving the 1955 Annual Patsy Award (Picture Animal Star of the Year) for his work in the MGM movie, "It's A Dog's Life". Accepting the award from B. Dean Clanton, president of the American Humane Association, is Wildfire's co-star, Jarma Lewis, with Dr. W. W. Young, Western regional AHA director, looking on. In real life "Wildfire" was Cadence Glacier, C. D., bred and owned by Lillian Koehler.

Graduation Day, 1954, for what is believed to be the largest number of Bull Terriers ever entered in one Obedience class. Trainer, William R. Koehler. Back row, l. to r.: Jack Reddick's Serenade's Casey Jones, Marilyn Reddick's Serenade's Song of Songs and Lillian Ritchell's Serenade's Button and Bows. Front row, Katy Ickis' Glorycady's Star of Even and Jill Bradshaw's Cadence Clown.

22

Conditioning, Grooming and Training

ONE of our great handlers once said, "Give me a square dog with a good coat, and in three hours I'll carve you out a top Kerry." That is true in many breeds, where the professional can do a trimming job that will cover up a host of faults and make a dog look far better than he actually is. It is not, however, true of a Bull Terrier. Nothing can be done to hide his structure and type—but he can be groomed and handled so as to enable him to put his best foot forward.

Bear in mind that the judge must base his evaluation on the dog as he is presented—not on how the dog might look if his owner had shown greater concern as to conditioning and grooming before entering the ring.

In preparing a Bull Terrier for show, the first thing to do is to get him in good, hard condition, with the glow of health in his skin, a sparkle in his eye, and the gloss in his coat that comes from proper feeding—a gloss like the glitter of freshly fallen snow when the sun slants on it.

Granted health and good condition as a foundation, the next thing to do is to get him clean. There is nothing like a lukewarm bath with mild soap, a good bit of block blueing in the water, and elbow grease. Some do not put the blueing in the washing water, but use it as a rinse; if block blueing is used, it can even be so dark as to streak the dog a bit, for this will come out with a thorough toweling.

After the dog has been well dried with a towel, plenty of chalk or other whitening agent can be worked into his coat. This accomplishes two things: First, it helps to dry the coat, since the chalk soaks up moisture. Second, if the dog's coat gets soiled later, the chalk coating on the hair makes it much easier to brush out the dirt after he has arrived at the show. Incidentally, I like a muslin or linen show coat for the dog, as it not only helps to keep him clean but also helps to make his coat lie flat.

Either before or after washing, there are a minimum of three places where the dog's hair must be trimmed. First, the long whiskers on the muzzle and over each eye. Second, the half circle in front of each ear. Third, the tail must be trimmed underneath and at the sides so that it tapers nicely. A special grooming razor or a stripping comb is good for this trimming of the tail. Curved scissors are excellent for the ears, and straight scissors for the other trimming. That is the limit of the trimming that can be safely attempted by an amateur.

A professional will trim three other places: the rear of the thighs, where there are long and somewhat unsightly hairs; along the line of the tuck-up, so that it will look cleaner; and, if the neck hair is too long he will use thinning shears or a stripping comb to get a cleaner look.

At the show the entire dog can be rubbed down with a medium sandpaper which smooths off the coat; this is also very helpful in giving the final finish to the tail. Then the dog should be given a thorough brushing to remove all chalk. Finally, a coat dressing may be used to give a final finish.

The head may then be chalked a bit, and the chalk rubbed in well, working with the hair and not against it. Feet and legs may be given an extra dab of chalk, especially the feet, and the dog is then ready for the ring. *But remember that if you use too much chalk, your dog may be disqualified.*

The foregoing will give a newcomer a fair idea of the basic principles in making up a Bull Terrier for show. However, there are some things, some tricks of the trade, that cannot be easily explained in writing. The serious newcomer will do well to go to a professional handler experienced with Bull Terriers and pay him a fee to be shown just how to make up a Bull Terrier. Because this is his business, a handler can generally convey more knowledge than can a breeder-exhibitor. That is also true of the actual handling of the dog in the ring. After a person has shown his dog a few times so that he knows what show procedure is all about and can ask intelligent questions, it is well worthwhile to take a few lessons from a professional handler.

Before entering competition, the owner should train his dog to obey simple basic commands, so that the dog may be readily controlled in the ring as well as at home. The Bull Terrier has six characteristics that must be taken into consideration when one starts to train him for home obedience or for the show ring:

—*He is highly intelligent.*
—*He is anxious to please.*
—*He is unusually sensitive.*
—*He is very determined.*
—*He craves human companionship and attention.*
—*He thrives on praise.*

The whole theory of training a Bull Terrier successfully, so that he enjoys the training and the fruits therof, is simply this: One must be clear in his own understanding of what the dog is expected to do, and how to explain it to the dog, with patience enough to overcome the dog's determination not to do what is wanted, and an encouraging kindness that never fails regardless of the provocation.

There is little that can be said about one's conduct in the show ring itself—that can best be learned from experience. However, there are several pointers which may be of help. One is to make sure that your dog always has proper footing; don't let him stand facing down hill or with his front legs in a hole. If he does not like to gait over a particular spot, avoid it even if you have to request the permission of the judge to do so. And always keep one eye on your dog and the other on the judge. This is no time to exchange pleasantries with a friend seated at the ringside. There is no telling

Another view of the whelping pen described on Page 168.

After whelping. Use heavy muslin. Let bitch stand
on muslin and mark for holes through which legs
will go. Tear the sides down part way into strips,
and tie over the back. Tighten each day to bring
the breasts back to shape.

238

when a judge will glance at your dog, especially if he has been somewhat impressed by it, and continued good showmanship is likely to take one higher than if the judge sees the dog standing out at shoulders, cow-hocked, or sagging aimlessly in the middle. Even if the judge is not influenced, show every single minute until the ribbons are actually handed out.

Another thing, let your dog show himself. Don't use a competitor's dog to spark yours. If the handler is smart, he won't let you do it—unless it is just the thing he needs to better his chances of beating you.

On the whole, I am pretty well convinced that judges do the best they can in the light of their knowledge and experience. However, no judge likes to have an exhibitor double-cross him by showing the winning dog well in the breed, and then going into the Group with the feeling, "I'll never do anything in the Group and I'm just here so that the breed will be represented"—and acting accordingly. Far better to stay out altogether. He'll be better off sharing a drink with one of his fellow exhibitors.

Twice I have put a dog to the top, once an Airedale and once a Staffordshire, only to have them mishandled in the Group. Although I always put up the dog that in my own opinion was the best one being shown under me, I can't find it in my heart to blame the professional who will put down the better dog to one that he knews will be handled properly in the Group.

The owner-handler who shames a judge by allowing his dog to show himself so as to exhibit all the faults in the breed is not doing any good to the breed, to himself, to his dog, or to the judge who has given him top billing and on whose choice he should try to reflect credit, instead of giving the spectators cause to say, "How on earth did he ever put up that dog! Why, he had some good ones there." Give your dog your best, every single instant, and don't ever let either him or the judge down. Only by doing so have you any business in the ring at all.

The author moving Davy Crockett of Ernicor in the Terrier Group competition at Westminster Kennel Club, Madison Square Garden 1956.

WHITE BULL TERRIER CHAMPIONS (AKC)—since 1960

1960
CH. DULAC BLENDED OF KEARBY
  (Kearby Kihikihi ex Crescent Catamount)
CH. KENTGATES MAYFLOWER
  (Ch. Sun Burst ex Kentgates Clover Bloom)
CH. BEDFORD'S DAUNTLESS BEAUTY II
  (Ch. Silverwood Top Grade ex Ch. Bedford's Future)
CH. SONATA OF MONTY-AYR
  (Vanguard of Monty-Ayr ex Ch. Moon Mood of Monty-Ayr)
CH. SNOW STORM OF COOLYN HILL
  (Ch. Kashdowd's White Rock of Coolyn Hill
   ex Coolyn Tavern Maid)
CH. SILVERWOOD EASTER BONNET
  (Ch. Phidgity Shepherd Boy of Lenster
   ex Ch. Silverwood Snippet)
CH. MELTDOWN MOTH
  (Ormandy Souperlative Snowflash ex Souperlative Silvertan)

1961
CH. TAP DANCER OF MONTY-AYR
  (Vanguard of Monty-Ayr ex Ch. Moon Mood of Monty-Ayr)
CH. BRAMBLEMERE GAY CAROLYNDA
  (Meltdown Moonraker ex Bramblemere Sweet Ruth)
CH. PRIMA BALLERINA OF MONTY-AYR
  (Vanguard of Monty-Ayr ex Ch. Moon Mood of Monty-Ayr)
CH. SNOW KING OF MONTY-AYR
  (Ch. Dancing Master of Monty-Ayr
   ex Ch. Tap Dancer of Monty-Ayr)
CH. WHITE CAVALIER OF MONTY-AYR
  (Ch. The Sphinx of Monty-Ayr ex Dulac Kearby's Jennie Wren)
CH. PALLADIUM JILL OF COOLYN HILL
  (Ch. Kashdowd's White Rock of Coolyn Hill
   ex Ch. Phidgity Pearly Glint)
CH. SILVERWOOD MRS. PEPPER
  (Ch. Silverwood Top Grade ex Starlight Duchess)
CH. CHALLENGE OF MONTY-AYR
  (Ch. Dancing Master of Monty-Ayr
   ex Ch. Black Witch of Monty-Ayr)
CH. HIGHBURN ANANDEL
  (Fingalian Fiery Cross ex Kilsae White Queen)

1962
CH. DAINTY JANE
  (Ch. Dulac Blended of Kearby ex Silverwood Dulac Spoonbill)

241

1962 (continued)

CH. SILVERWOOD PRINCE VALIANT
 (Ch. Phidgity Shepherd Boy of Lenster
  ex Ch. Silverwood Snippet)
CH. ROMBUS ANDANTE
 (Souperlative Brinhead ex Romany Rosemullion)
CH. SNOW QUEEN OF MONTY-AYR
 (Ch. Dancing Master of Monty-Ayr
  ex Ch. Tap Dancer of Monty-Ayr)
CH. EL DORADO OF MONTY-AYR
 (Ch. Dancing Master of Monty-Ayr
  ex Ch. Snow Queen of Monty-Ayr)
CH. RUNNING BEAR OF MINGO
 (Ch. Dancing Master of Monty-Ayr
  ex Ch. Atomic Blonde of Monty-Ayr)

1963

CH. WHITE EAGLE OF MINGO
 (Snow King of Monty-Ayr ex
  Indian Summer of Monty-Ayr)
CH. LOVELAND'S WHITE TIDE
 (Hollyhey Perfection ex Ch. Symphony II of Monty-Ayr)
CH. PHOEBE SNOW OF WESTMEATH
 (Ch. Phidgity Shepherd Boy of Lenster
  ex Ch. Abraxas Athena of Westmeath)
CH. WHITE PETUNIA OF LA MIRADA
 (Ch. Mars Grenadier ex Jezebel of La Mirada)
CH. BEDFORD'S LOVELY LADY
 (Ch. Silverwood Top Grade
  ex Ch. Bedford's Dauntless Beauty II)
CH. SILVERWOOD DULAC SPOONBILL
 (The Conqueror of Kearby ex Dulac Crossbill)
CH. SILVERWOOD LOCKET
 (Ch. Sun Burst ex Ch. Silverwood Cameo)
CH. OLD IRONSIDES OF MONTY-AYR
 (Ch. Snow King of Monty-Ayr ex Ch. Moon Mood of Monty-Ayr)
CH. LOVELAND'S EGYPTIAN PRINCESS
 (Ch. White Cavalier of Monty-Ayr
  ex Ch. Symphony II of Monty-Ayr)
CH. LOVELAND'S EGYPTIAN CAVALIER
 (Ch. White Cavalier of Monty-Ayr
  ex Ch. Symphony II of Monty-Ayr)
CH. PHIDGITY PHLYING FANCY
 (Ormandy Souperlative Princeling ex Loravon Snow Belle)
CH. KRACKTON ROBIN OF WENTWOOD
 (Romany Robin Goodfellow ex Phidgity Flashlight of Wentwood)
CH. LUCKY STRIKE OF MONTY-AYR
 (Ch. Dancing Master of Monty-Ayr
  ex Ch. Snow Queen of Monty-Ayr)

242

1963 (continued)
CH. DRUM MAJOR OF MONTY-AYR
(Ch. Snow King of Monty-Ayr ex Ch. Tap Dancer of Monty-Ayr)

1964
CH. BEDFORD'S LADY PENELOPE
(Ch. Dancing Master of Monty-Ayr
ex Ch. Bedford's Rather Lovely)
CH. SILVERWOOD SIGNET
(Ch. Highburn Anandel ex Silverwood Locket)
CH. HARPER'S HUNTSMAN
(Ch. Phidgity Phlasher of Lenster
ex Ch. Harper's Heather Girl)
CH. WHITE GARDENIA OF LA MIRADA
(Ch. Holcroft Squire Robin ex Ch. Holcroft Blossom)
CH. HOLCROFT SQUIRE ROBIN
(Ch. Krackton Robin of Wentwood ex Holcroft Miss Bimbo)
CH. SHERIDAN'S BROWN-EYED SUSAN
(Ch. Red Fire of Camaloch
ex Ch. Westmeath's Classy Chassis)
CH. WHITE DIAMOND OF ONSLAUT
(Ch. Onslaut's David ex Bonnie of Onslaut)
CH. TOP SERGEANT OF MONTY-AYR
(Ch. Dancing Master of Monty-Ayr
ex Ch. Snow Queen of Monty-Ayr)
CH. WHITE CAMELIA OF LA MIRADA
(Ch. Mars Grenadier ex Jezebell of La Mirada)
CH. TEDDY'S BRUMMIES BOY
(Woodcock of Brun ex Ch. Melodious of Brun)
CH. WILSMERE ROSILLA
(Oldlane Swainhouse Superfire ex Wilsmere Lizilla)
CH. ORMANDY'S ARDEE REGAL DUKE
(Ormandy's Souperlative Princeling
ex Ardee Really Desirable)
CH. SILVERWOOD BIT O'MUSLIN
(Ch. Highburn Anandel ex Ch. Silverwood Snippet)
CH. HARVEY'S COOK OF BAYOU PARK
(Leprechaun Harvey ex Balechin Banshee)

1965
CH. ORMANDY'S WESTWARD HO
(Ormandy Souperlative Bar Sinister
ex Ormandy's Duncannon Double Two)
CH. GOLDFINGER
(Ormandy's Ben of Highthorpe ex Valkyries White Clown)
CH. BERBAN'S DERVISH OF MONTY-AYR
(Ch. Dancing Master of Monty-Ayr
ex Ch. Moon Mood of Monty-Ayr)

243

1965 (continued)
CH. ONSLAUT'S PANDORA
 (Snowflash of Monty-Ayr ex Bonnie of Onslaut)
CH. WILHELM'S TORY
 (Onslaut's Tonie ex Onslaut's Pandora)
CH. SHERIDAN'S GENTLEMAN JOHN
 (Parade of Monty-Ayr ex Sheridan's Brown-Eyed Susan)
CH. LOVELAND'S WINDY McLAIN
 (Ch. White Cavalier of Monty-Ayr
 ex Ch. Symphony II of Monty-Ayr)
CH. DULY'S WHITE MARDI GRAS
 (Gordon's Tristan ex Rosebud of Monty-Ayr)
CH. MIGHTY MOE OF MONTY-AYR
 (Ch. Dancing Master of Monty-Ayr
 ex Bonanza of Monty-Ayr)
CH. FANCY PRANCE OF CURCHCREST
 (Ch. Mars Grenadier ex Jezebel of La Mirada)
CH. HOLCROFT KELLY
 (Ch. Krackton Robin of Wentwood
 ex Holcroft Chorus Girl)
CH. ONSLAUT'S SCARAMOUCHE
 (Onslaut"s Tonie ex Onslaut's Pandora)
CH. PAINTED ROSE OF LA MIRADA
 (Ch. Mars Grenadier ex Jezebel of La Mirada)
CH. SWAINHOUSE SPORTSMAN
 (Souperlative Masta Plasta ex Swainhouse Willow Wren)
CH. BEJOBO'S MERRY SUNSHINE
 (Willson's Morning Star ex Valiant Sprite)
CH. LE MARQUIS DE SCARAMOUCHE
 (Onslaut's Scaramouche ex Ch. Silverwood Easter Bonnet)
CH. LORD COBBOLT OF DREADNOUGHT
 (Ch. Krackton Robin of Wentwood
 ex Lady Guinevere of Melrose)
CH. RINGO STAR OF LA MIRADA
 (White Tornado of La Mirada ex Ch. Holcroft Blossom)
CH. SILVERWOOD TALISMAN
 (Ch. Krackton Robin of Wentwood ex Silverwood Charm)
CH. MASTERPIECE OF MONTY-AYR
 (Ch. Dancing Master of Monty-Ayr
 ex Bonanza of Monty-Ayr)
CH. PUSSY GALORE
 (Ormandy's Ben of Highthorpe ex Valkyries White Clown)
CH. VALKYRIE MILK TRAY
 (Romany Romantic Vision ex Duncannon One Spot)
CH. LADY GUINEVERE OF MELROSE
 (Ch. Phidgity Shepherd Boy of Lenster
 ex Monica of Melrose)

1965 (continued)
CH. SUPERLATIVE DOLL OF MONTY-AYR
(Ch. Dancing Master of Monty-Ayr
 ex Ch. Moon Mood of Monty-Ayr)

1966
CH. BRAMBLEMERE DUBLE TRUBLE
(Oldland Swainhouse Superfine ex Wilsmere Alice)
CH. LADY CHARMAIN OF DREADNOUGHT
(Ch. Lord Cobbolt of Dreadnought ex Silverwood Ghost)
CH. TIGER LILY OF STORM HILLS
(White Tornado of La Mirada
 ex Ch. Painted Rose of La Mirada)
CH. DULY's CAJUN PRINCESS
(Gordon's Tristan ex Rosebud of Monty-Ayr)
CH. WILD IS THE WIND IN LA MIRADA
(Ch. Krackton Robin of Wentwood
 ex Ch. White Gardenia of La Mirada)
CH. SOUPERLATIVE SPICE OF HESKATHANE
(Ormandy's Thunderflash ex Souperlative Crepe Suzette)
CH. CONAMOR PRIX DE SCARAMOUCHE
(Ch. Swainhouse Sportsman ex Ch. Ormandy's Westward Ho)
CH. LA·MIRADA'S WAR PAINT
(Ch. Krackton Robin of Wentwood
 ex Ch. Gardenia of La Mirada)
CH. LORD DOWNY OF DREADNOUGHT
(Krackton Kwait ex Ch. Lady Guinevere of Melrose)
CH. MELTDOWN MARK
(Ormandy's Ben of Highthorpe ex Meltdown Summer Place)
CH. SILVERWOOD SIELOK SPARKLER
(Agates Flashpoint ex Bella of Ricodi)
CH. ORMANDY'S BURSON'S BOUNTY
(Souperlative Sea Captain ex Burson's Benita)
CH. THE BARON OF HIGHLAND PARK
(Onslaut's Scaramouche ex Ch. Silverwood Easter Bonnet)
CH. HOLCROFT LEADING LADY
(Franda's Brandy Snap ex Mist of the Morn)

.1967
CH. HARPER'S RICKARDO
(Souperlative Acetylene ex Harper's Highstar)
CH. CONAMOR TAYLORWOOD LIKE LOVE
(Ch. Swainhouse Sportsman ex Ch. Ormandy's Westward Ho)
CH. CONAMOR'S HOOLIGAN OF HI-LO
(Ch. Swainhouse Sportsman ex Ch. Ormandy's Westward Ho)
CH. LEWISFIELD'S POUIQUETTE
(Ch. Goldfinger ex Ch. Rombus Andante)

245

1967 (continued)
CH. CONAMOR KID OF LA MIRADA
 (Ch. Swainhouse Sportsman ex Ch. Ormandy's Westward Ho)
CH. BONNET'S LOVELY LADY
 (Ch. Onslaut's Scaramouche ex Ch. Silverwood Easter Bonnet)
CH. SILVERWOOD AGATES MR. PICKWICK
 (Ormandy's Thunderflash ex Agates Lotus Elite)
CH. DORLONS ROBIN OF HI-LO
 (White Tornado of La Mirada ex Summer Queen of Hi-Lo)
CH. KILLER JOE
 (Ch. Krackton Robin of Wentwood ex Kowhai Lottie)
CH. LA MIRADA'S HAPPY HOOLIGAN
 (White Tornado of La Mirada ex Blossom Time in La Mirada)
CH. BLACKEYED SUSAN OF LA MIRADA
 (Ch. Mighty Moe of Monty Ayr ex Honey Suckle of La Mirada)
CH. SILVERWOOD SERENADE
 (Ormandy's Thunderflash ex Silverwood Sturdee Romancy)
CH. ROBIN HOOD OF NOTTINGHAM
 (Ch. Bramblemere Duble Truble ex Ch. Valkyries Milk Tray)
CH. TAREYTON OF WOODLAND HILLS
 (White Tornado of La Mirada ex White Tasmin of La Mirada)
CH. KAYWANA SAMANTHA
 ·(Ch. Krackton Robin of Wentwood ex Kowhai Fantasai)
CH. DEPUTY COMMANDER OF LENSTER
 (Ormandy Souperlative Bar Sinister ex Rombus Allegro)
CH. LADY NELLE OF DREADNOUGHT
 (Krackton Kwait ex Lady Priscilla of Dreadnought)

1968
CH. SOUPERLATIVE SPACE QUEEN
 (Ormandy's Ben of Highthorpe ex Souperlative Cocoa)
CH. WHITE SQUIRE OF SCARAMOUCHE
 (Ch. Onslauts Scaramouche ex Ch. Silverwood Easter Bonnet)
CH. SILVERWOOD MONKERY'S CAVIAR
 (Ormandy Souperlative Bar Sinister
 ex Monkery's Snowflake of Ormandy)
CH. STURDEE WILSMERE CHRISTABELLE
 (Ormandy's Thunderflash ex Wilsmer Lizilla)
CH. CONAMOR'S JOY OF HI-LO
 (Ch. Swainhouse Sportsman ex Ch. Ormandy's Westward Ho)
CH. SCARAMOUCHE'S SOUPER SPHINX
 (Ch. Swainhouse Sportsman
 ex Ch. Conamor Prix de Scaramouche)
CH. BANBURY BRICK
 (Ch. Bramblemere Duble Truble ex Ch. Valkyries Milk Tray)
CH. BARCLAY'S ALGONQUIN QUEEN
 (Chatsworth Zephyr ex Queen of Grand River Valley)

246

1968 (continued)
CH. CORDOVA'S MASTER PLASTERER
 (Ch. Masterpiece of Monty-Ayr ex Red Moon of Mingo)
CH. LOVELAND'S HAPPY DAYS
 (Ch. White Cavalier of Monty-Ayr
 ex Ch. Symphony II of Monty-Ayr)
CH. WILTON'S PEEPER
 (Ch. Harper's Huntsman ex Ch. Barnes' Brigit)
CH. HY-LO'S MR. ERNIE
 (Ch. Ormandy's Burson's Bounty ex Conamor's Joy of Hi-Lo)

 1969
CH. HOLCROFT QUEENIE'S NIPPY GIRL
 (Ch. Krackton Robin of Wentwood ex Holcroft Silver Queen)
CH. TURNEY'S TAREYTON
 (Robin The Hood of La Mirada ex Holcroft Leading Lady)
CH. AUDACIEUX IRON DUKE
 (Ch. Conamor Kid of La Mirada
 ex Silverwood's Daffodowndilly)
CH. PANDA'S DELIGHT OF SOHNRIZE
 (Ch. Dreadnought's Mr. Panda ex Valkyrie Dairy Box)
CH. SHERIDAN'S PANDA
 (Parade of Monty-Ayr
 ex Sheridan's Brown-Eyed Susan)
CH. PATHENS PRINCESS ALICE
 (Ch. Commander of Monty-Ayr ex Ch. Holcroft Leading Lady)
CH. BEJOBO'S JACK FROST
 (Ch. Conamor's Hooligan of Hi-Lo ex Night Star of Hi-Lo)
CH. PANDA'S HEIRESS OF SOHNRIZE
 (Ch. Dreadnought's Mr. Panda ex Valkyrie Dairy Box)
CH. GORA'S PAS
 (Robin The Hood of La Mirada ex Holcroft Leading Lady)
CH. KASHDOWD BOUNCE
 (Romany Rover Scout ex Valkyrie Gemini)
CH. HOLCROFT LADY JOAN
 (Ch. Silverwood Agates Mr. Pickwick ex Holcroft Hasty Clown)
CH. MELTDOWN RED ADMIRAL
 (Maerdy Master Mariner ex Meltdown Morning Star)
CH. TRIPLE TRUBLE OF SOHNRIZE
 (Ch. Bramblemere Duble Truble ex Valkyrie Dairy Box)
CH. CORDOVA'S TEMPEST STORM
 (Ch. Masterpiece of Monty-Ayr ex Auspro Terros of Cordova)
CH. CRESTMERE BETTINA
 (Wilsmere's Dauntless ex Ch. Wilsmere Rosilla)
CH. DREADNOUGHT PEPPERMINT
 (Ch. Lord Cobbolt of Dreadnought
 ex Lady Penelope of Dreadnought)

247

1969 (continued)
CH. HERCULEAN TERROR
  (Ch. Conamor Kid of La Mirada ex Turney's Tareyton)
CH. HIS NIBS OF BROBAR
  (Brobar Booster ex Brobar Caramia)
CH. PUTNAMVILLE SAILOR
  (Ch. Krackton Robin of Wentwood ex Holcroft Silver Queen)
CH. SUN WAY'S STORMY TERRY
  (Holcroft Hurricane ex Kentgates Bonnie)
CH. HOLCROFT ARCHER
  (Ch. Krackton Robin of Wentwood ex Holcroft Kowhai Lottie)
CH. LA MIRADA'S MARKSMAN
  (Ch. Swainhouse Sportsman ex La Mirada's Canterbury Bell)
CH. PALOOKA'S PAL
  (Ch. Krackton Robin of Wentwood
  ex Kandy Kisses of Monty-Ayr)

1970
CH. CARLINGS SOLITAIRE
  (Ch. Holcroft Diplomat ex Pollyanna of Monty-Ayr)
CH. DAFFODOWNDILLY'S GRETCHEN
  (Ch. Conamor Kid of La Mirada
  ex Silverwood's Daffodowndilly)
CH. SILVERWOOD FIRE BELLE CLAPPER
  (Ormandy's Thunderflash ex Silverwood Sturdee Romancy)
CH. CONAMOR BARNEY BRINDLEAR
  (Petrikov Damos of Lewisfield ex Ch. Ormandy's Westward Ho)
CH. FROSTINE EL'LEON OF CORDOVA
  (Ch. Masterpiece of Monty-Ayr ex Auspro Terros of Cordova)
CH. LA MIRADA'S GALAXI
  (Jolly Good of La Mirada
  ex Ch. Blackeyed Susan of La Mirada)
CH. PANDA'S SLASHER OF SOHNRIZE
  (Ch. Dreadnought's Mr. Panda ex Valkyrie Dairy Box)
CH. BOLD RULER OF MONTY-AYR
  (Redigo of Monty-Ayr ex Wendy of Monty-Ayr)
CH. HIGHLAND'S CONSTANT HARP
  (Ch. White Squire of Scaramouche ex Delantero Double Quest)
CH. KEARBY MAXWELL'S GOLD DUST
  (Ch. Geham Gold Label ex Ardee Radiant Delight)
CH. BELLET TERRE'S PATIENCE
  (Ch. Killer Joe ex Crestmere Bettina)
CH. COMANCHE OF UPEND
  (Langville Pilot Officer ex Ormandy's Caunsul Charm)

248

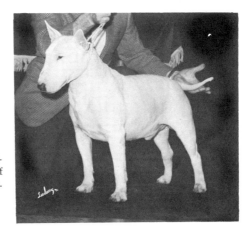

Ch. Conamors Hooligan of Hi-Lo, top West Coast winner of 1969. Owned by Mr. and Mrs. Roy Johnson.

Ch. Little Willows Young Scalp, a California star of the 1950 era. Owned by Eleanor Griffin.

Ch. Nightriders Rasteau, another West Coast winner in the '50s.

249

COLORED BULL TERRIER CHAMPIONS (AKC)—since 1960

1960
CH. DULAC KEARBY'S JENNIE WREN
(Ch. Dulac Heathlands Commander ex Kearby's Kakapo)

1961
CH. BRINDLE CHIEF OF MINGO
(Vindicator of Monty-Ayr
ex Indian Summer of Monty-Ayr)
CH. LITTLE WILLOWS BABY DOLL
(Ch. Little Willows Young Scalp
ex Pryor's Prickly Pear of Tartary)

1962
CH. TARTARY DULAC REDSHANK
(Dulac Osprey ex Kearby Kororareka)
CH. DULAC COCK OF THE ROCK
(Beechhouse Snow Vision ex Dulac Barn Owl)
CH. INDIAN SUMMER OF MONTY-AYR
(Ch. The Sphinx of Monty-Ayr ex Ch. Tregony Tuba)
CH. LITTLE WILLOWS WILTON
(Davocal's Defender ex Ch. Little Willows Baby Doll)

1963
No Champions

1964
CH. BARNES BRIGET
(Ch. Fredella's Prince Charming
ex Little Willows Lolita)
CH. COMMANDER OF MONTY-AYR
(Ch. Dancing Master of Monty-Ayr
ex Caprice of Monty-Ayr)
CH. VON BRUENS BANDIT BOLD
(Ch. Little Willows Brindiboy ex Von Bruens Juliana)
CH. HOLCROFT DAWN OF TOMORROW
(Ch. Krackton Robin of Wentwood ex Ch. Holcroft Blossom)

1965
CH. HOLCROFT BLOSSOM HARRISON
(Ch. Krackton Robin of Wentwood ex Ch. Holcroft Blossom)
CH. ROMBUS ASTRONAUT OF LENSTER
(Souperlative Brinhead ex Romany Rosemullion)
CH. HERMES LIKEABLE LUKE
(Nicholas ex Pennywoods Ha'Penny)

250

1966
CH. CRESSWOOD LORD DERBY
 (Dulac Buff Rock ex Miss I. Q. of Monty-Ayr, CD)
CH. LA MIRADA'S STERLING KNIGHT
 (Gypsy Baron of La Mirada
  ex Ch. White Camelia of La Mirada)
CH. PRINCESS BAMBI
 (Ch. Krackton Robin of Wentwood ex Holcroft Chorus Girl)
CH. HEADMASTER OF LA MIRADA
 (White Tornado of La Mirada ex Ch. Holcroft Blossom)
CH. GAY CHERIE OF LA MIRADA
 (Ch. Commander of Monty-Ayr ex High Time of Monty-Ayr)

1967
CH. HOLCROFT DIPLOMAT
 (Ch. Krackton Robin of Wentwood ex Holcroft Red Gauntlet)
CH. BILMAR'S MOON SHADOW
 (Ch. Silverwood Signet ex Winsted Libby Coy)
CH. DREADNOUGHT'S MR. PANDA
 (Krackton Kwait ex Lady Priscilla of Dreadnought)
CH. HARPER'S HOLDFAST
 (Starline of Lenster ex Harper's Hyacinth)
CH. SEAWEED OF LENSTER
 (Ch. Rombus Astronaut of Lenster ex Bambola of Lenster)
CH. ABRAXAS ACE OF ACES
 (Ormandy's Ben of Highthorpe ex Abraxas Alvina)
CH. WILTON'S ORION
 (Ch. Harper's Huntsman ex Ch. Barnes Briget)

1968
CH. THE SWINGER OF HY-LO
 (Ch. Conamor's Hooligan of Hi Lo ex Night Star of Hi Lo)
CH. TINA GINA OF MONTY-AYR
 (Ch. Commander of Monty-Ayr ex Bonanza of Monty-Ayr)
CH. LA MIRADA'S HOT MOON
 (Meltdown Moonshiner ex Harper's Hilarity)
CH. LITTLE WILLOWS HAPPINESS
 (Ch. Harper's Huntsman ex Ch. Barnes Briget)
CH. GYPSY MAGIC IN LA MIRADA
 (Gypsy Baron of La Mirada ex White Jasmine of La Mirada)
CH. AUGUST BEAUTY OF MONTY-AYR
 (Ch. Commander of Monty-Ayr ex Bonanza of Monty-Ayr)
CH. LADYBIRD OF MONTY-AYR
 (Ch. Commander of Monty-Ayr ex Bonanza of Monty-Ayr)
CH. POINSETTIA OF LA MIRADA
 (Ch. Commander of Monty-Ayr ex Ch. Holcroft Kelly)
CH. DAVID'S SPENCER SNUFF
 (Willson's Morning Star ex Frisco Folly of Monty-Ayr)

251

1968 (continued)
CH. ROUGHRIDER OF MONTY-AYR
(Redigo of Monty-Ayr ex Wendy of Monty-Ayr)
CH. GINGER CRUMPET, C.D.
(White Tornado of La Mirada ex Lady Crumpet of La Mirada)
CH. GREYSTROKE OF DREADNOUGHT
(Krackton Kwait ex Lady Priscilla of Dreadnought)
CH. SOUPERBA BRINSPOT
(Ch. Krackton Robin of Wentwood
 ex Valkyrie's White Clown)

1969
CH. SCARAMOUCHE'S TANFASTIC
(Ch. Conamor Kid of La Mirada
 ex Dazzling Holly of La Mirada)
CH. DAZZLING HOLLY OF LA MIRADA
(Ch. Commander of Monty-Ayr ex Ch. Holcroft Kelly)
CH. LA MIRADA'S RED COAT
(Ch. Swainhouse Sportsman ex Harper's Higlow)
CH. ONSLAUT'S ENCHILADA
(Ch. Abraxas Ace of Aces ex Onslaut's Sherry)
CH. AGATE'S BRONZINO
(Ch. Abraxas Ace of Aces ex Agates Lotus Elite)
CH. PANDA'S FLAME OF SOHNRIZE
(Ch. Dreadnought's Mr. Panda ex Valkyrie Dairy Box)
CH. COMMODORE OF MONTY-AYR
(Redigo of Monty-Ayr ex Wendy of Monty-Ayr)
CH. GOLDEN GIRL OF ENCHANTED LAKE
(Onslaut's Tonie ex Black Pearl of Camaloch)
CH. HOLCROFT LADY TAMATHA
(Ch. Krackton Robin of Wentwood
 ex Holcroft Red Gauntlet)
CH. CARLINGS MINNIE THE MASHER
(Franda's Brandy Snap ex Pollyanna of Monty-Ayr)
CH. HY-LO'S BATMAN
(White Knight of Lenster ex Ch. The Swinger of Hy-Lo)
CH. RAWHIDE OF LA MIRADA
(Ch. La Mirada's Hot Moon ex Sun Way's Little Rhody)

1970
CH. DREADNOUGHT'S NEMESIS
(Ch. Dreadnought's Mr. Panda ex Valkyrie Dairy Box)
CH. BROADSIDE BEGONE
(Ch. Goldfinger ex Turney's Siren)
CH. HY-LO'S CORDOVAN ENTERPRISE
(White Knight of Lenster ex Ch. The Swinger of Hy-Lo)
CH. HY-LO'S BLOSSOM
(Ch. Abraxas Ace of Aces ex Conamor's Joy of Hi-Lo)

1970 (continued)
CH. LA MIRADA'S MOONLIGHT N' ROSES
(Songleader of La Mirada ex La Mirada's Rosebud)
CH. WILTON'S BRUCE
(Wilton's Christopher ex Wilton's Chili)
CH. AQUARIUS OF MINGO
(Thunder of Mingo ex Ch. August Beauty of Monty-Ayr)

Ch. Headmaster of La Mirada, a 1966 champion
West Coast winner. Owner, James P. DeMangos.

Ch. Westmeath's Reliance, California
Specialty winner of the 1950s.

Ch. Little Willows Happiness, 1968 champion daughter of Ch. Harpers Huntsman
ex Ch. Barnes Brigit.

253

Winsted's Bedford Belle, C.D., C.D.X., U.D., U.D.T., the first Bull Terrier to attain the Utility Dog degree. Owned by Dr. Harry L. Otis, optometrist.

Ch. Duncan Willie of Camaloch, C.D., C.D.X.

Eng. Ch. Romany Righteous Wrath, C.D.

Diamond Jim Brady of Ernicor, C.D., C.D.X., pictured scoring perfect score in C.D.X.—first time ever for a Bull Terrier. Owner, Frank Neff. Judge, Mrs. Alva McColl.

254

OBEDIENCE TITLE WINNERS
(1959 to 1969)

1959:   Serenade's Rigolette, CD

1960:   Poticas Patch, CD

1961:   White Ash of Oaktree, CDX

1963:   Winsted Viva, CD
        Winsted Michele, CD

1964:   Lady Iva of Broreed, CD
        Miss IQ of Monty-Ayr, CD
        Cadence Lady Chatterly, CD

1966:   Winsted Michele, CDX
        Cadence Lady Chatterly, CDX
        Ch. Souperlative Doll of Monty-Ayr, CD

1967:   Lavender Timbeau of Monty-Ayr, CD
        Blake's Heather O' The Isle, CD, CDX
        Jancey of Macshaven, CD
        Ginger Crumpet, CD

1968:   Broadside Badger, CD
        Silverwood Let's Take A Chance, CD

1969:   Wilsmere Pixie of Palladium, CD

BIBLIOGRAPHY

ALL OWNERS of pure-bred dogs will benefit themselves and their dogs by enriching their knowledge of breeds and of canine care, training, breeding, psychology and other important aspects of dog management. The following list of books covers further reading recommended by judges, veterinarians, breeders, trainers and other authorities. Books may be obtained at the finer book stores and pet shops, or through Howell Book House Inc., publishers, New York, N.Y.

Breed Books

AFGHAN HOUND, Complete	Miller & Gilbert
AIREDALE, Complete	Edwards
ALASKAN MALAMUTE, Complete	Riddle & Seeley
BASSET HOUND, Complete	Braun
BEAGLE, Complete	Noted Authorities
BLOODHOUND, Complete	Brey & Reed
BOXER, Complete	Denlinger
BRITTANY SPANIEL, Complete	Riddle
BULLDOG, New Complete	Hanes
BULL TERRIER, New Complete	Eberhard
CAIRN TERRIER, Complete	Marvin
CHIHUAHUA, Complete	Noted Authorities
COLLIE, Complete	Official Publication of the
Collie Club of America	
DACHSHUND, The New	Meistrell
DOBERMAN PINSCHER, New	Walker
ENGLISH SETTER, New Complete	Tuck & Howell
ENGLISH SPRINGER SPANIEL, New	
Goodall & Gasow	
FOX TERRIER, New Complete	Silvernail
GERMAN SHEPHERD DOG, Complete	Bennett
GERMAN SHORTHAIRED POINTER, New	Maxwell
GOLDEN RETRIEVER, Complete	Fischer
GREAT DANE, New Complete	Noted Authorities
GREAT PYRENEES, Complete	Strang & Giffin
IRISH SETTER, New	Thompson
IRISH WOLFHOUND, Complete	Starbuck
KEESHOND, Complete	Peterson
LABRADOR RETRIEVER, Complete	Warwick
MINIATURE SCHNAUZER, Complete	Eskrigge
NEWFOUNDLAND, New Complete	Chern
NORWEGIAN ELKHOUND, New Complete	Wallo
OLD ENGLISH SHEEPDOG, Complete	Mandeville
PEKINGESE, Quigley Book of	Quigley
POMERANIAN, New Complete	Ricketts
POODLE, New Complete	Hopkins & Irick
POODLE CLIPPING AND GROOMING BOOK,	
Complete	Kalstone
PUG, Complete	Trullinger
PULI, Complete	Owen
ST. BERNARD, New Complete	
Noted Authorities, rev. Raulston	
SAMOYED, Complete	Ward
SCHIPPERKE, Official Book of	Root, Martin, Kent
SCOTTISH TERRIER, Complete	Marvin
SHETLAND SHEEPDOG, New	Riddle
SHIH TZU, The (English)	Dadds
SIBERIAN HUSKY, Complete	Demidoff
TERRIERS, The Book of All	Marvin
TOY DOGS, Kalstone Guide to Grooming All	
Kalstone	
TOY DOGS, All About	Ricketts
WEST HIGHLAND WHITE TERRIER,	
Complete	Marvin
WHIPPET, Complete	Pegram
YORKSHIRE TERRIER, Complete	
Gordon & Bennett	

Care and Training

DOG OBEDIENCE, Complete Book of	Saunders
NOVICE, OPEN AND UTILITY COURSES	Saunders
DOG CARE AND TRAINING, Howell	
Book of	Howell, Denlinger, Merrick
DOG CARE AND TRAINING FOR BOYS	
AND GIRLS	Saunders
DOG TRAINING FOR KIDS	Benjamin
DOG TRAINING, Koehler Method of	Koehler
GO FIND! Training Your Dog to Track	Davis
GUARD DOG TRAINING, Koehler Method of	
Koehler	
OPEN OBEDIENCE FOR RING, HOME	
AND FIELD, Koehler Method of	Koehler
SPANIELS FOR SPORT (English)	Radcliffe
SUCCESSFUL DOG TRAINING, The	
Pearsall Guide to	Pearsall
TRAIN YOUR OWN GUN DOG,	
How to	Goodall
TRAINING THE RETRIEVER	Kersley
TRAINING YOUR DOG TO WIN	
OBEDIENCE TITLES	Morsell
UTILITY DOG TRAINING, Koehler Method of	
Koehler	

Breeding

ART OF BREEDING BETTER DOGS, New	Onstott
HOW TO BREED DOGS	Whitney
HOW PUPPIES ARE BORN	Prine
INHERITANCE OF COAT COLOR	
IN DOGS	Little

General

COMPLETE DOG BOOK, The	
Official Pub. of American Kennel Club	
DOG IN ACTION, The	Lyon
DOG BEHAVIOR, New Knowledge of	
Pfaffenberger	
DOG JUDGING, Nicholas Guide to	Nicholas
DOG NUTRITION, Collins Guide to	Collins
DOG PSYCHOLOGY	Whitney
DOG STANDARDS ILLUSTRATED	
DOGSTEPS, Illustrated Gait at a Glance	Elliott
ENCYCLOPEDIA OF DOGS, International	
Dangerfield, Howell & Riddle	
JUNIOR SHOWMANSHIP HANDBOOK	
Brown & Mason	
SUCCESSFUL DOG SHOWING, Forsyth Guide to	
Forsyth	
TRIM, GROOM AND SHOW YOUR DOG,	
How to	Saunders
WHY DOES YOUR DOG DO THAT?	Bergman
WORLD OF SLED DOGS, From Siberia to	
Sport Racing	Coppinger
OUR PUPPY'S BABY BOOK (blue or pink)	